STEEL WRAPPED IN *Velvet*

An Integrated Approach to Healing, Moving From Trauma to Triumph

SONYA COOK

TABLE OF CONTENTS

ACKNOWLEDGEMENTS

First and foremost, I give honor to God and my Lord and Savior Jesus Christ; for with God all things are possible. I am grateful to all who participated in my research project. A heartfelt thank you to Calvary Baptist Church for their participation in the research project that led to the writing of this book. I thank all of those who mentored me throughout the years from undergraduate work to doctoral studies.

There was a moment in graduate school that has resonated with me for years. During my graduate studies at the Alliance Theological Seminary where I completed a reflection paper, we were instructed to read to our classmates as part of the assignment. Upon completing my reading, my professor thought for a moment, and said what came to him was *Steel Wrapped in Velvet*, from which comes the title of this book. Blessings to this Professor. I am grateful to the friends and associates who supported me with their prayers and words of encouragement.

A special thank you to my family, whose prayers, support, words of encouragement and affirmation continued to push me forward in meeting the purpose and plan that God has for my life. I am truly blessed to have a family that stands on God's word. And of course, a warm and loving thank you to my husband, for his steadfast and undying love for me, who supported me through each of my endeavors; and to my sons who cheered me on throughout this journey. May each page of this narrative bring glory to God.

INTRODUCTION:
THE PASTORAL
COUNSELOR AT A
GLANCE

reetings and blessing to you. I am grateful that you chose to read of my healing journey—a journey from a world of darkness and despair to a life of peace and joy, from a life void of purpose to a life fulfilled with purpose. My prayer is that my story not only serves as a testimony of my life journey, but also as an inspiration to you, the reader. No matter what life throws your way, you can survive; not only survive, but thrive in all that God has in store for you.

All those things that were meant for evil in my life, God turned it to be used for good. My life's journey as a survivor of physical, verbal, and sexual abuse set the stage for my role as a Pastoral Counselor and Licensed Marriage and Family Therapist (LMFT). My family dysfunction became one of the pathways to salvation through Jesus Christ. It also birthed a passion and conviction to help individuals and families dealing with dysfunctionality. As I once heard, *you cannot take anyone where you are not willing to go yourself.* It was through and by the Lord's strength that I ventured to go there. I journeyed through the aisle of darkness in search of the light of healing. As a Christian and counselor, my healing from the trauma of abuse not only came through Jesus Christ, but through psychotherapy as well.

Obtaining a certification in pastoral counseling and a masters in marriage and family therapy provided me with an understanding that faith and therapy are not mutually exclusive of each other. Another light bulb moment was that seeking therapy does not compromise one's faith. Becoming a pastoral counselor and obtaining a degree and licensure in marriage and family therapy proved to be advantageous to my private practice in bridging the gap between both disciplines. I discovered the use of both disciplines as an essential part of any pastoral care ministry and therapeutic process. Each discipline offers sound biblical theology, scriptures, and theory. This unique form of counseling provides the congregate/client with a holistic treatment plan, a holistic plan focusing on how an individual's personal relationships, i.e., family, patterns of behavior, and life choices interconnect with their presenting issues. This framework has become an essential part of my pastoral counseling and marriage and family therapy practice.

As a pastoral counselor/LMFT, I can attest to the effectiveness of an integrative approach that brings together the theological and psychological concepts into its framework. I can safely say that any pastoral care ministry or counseling ministry that offers this "dynamic duo" enhances the dynamic of the counseling/therapeutic experience.

Throughout these pages, I share not only the insights that I gained through my research, but also what a blessing this approach has been to me, my family, and the individuals and families that I serve. I pray that my story and my journey breathe the passion and conviction that I have for the very foundation of our world—the family.

THIS IS MY STORY
WITHOUT A SONG

One's journey would be much lighter
if the baggage of the past did not come with us.

I grew up in a large, extended family: father, mother, maternal grandmother, brothers, and sisters. I was told that my mother and father married at a very early age because my father was going into the armed services. Since my father was underage, his mother had to sign for him. My mom's reason for marrying early was that there was nothing else to do.

As a WW II veteran, my father shared stories of the war. These experiences probably contributed to the many nightmares and startled responses that he exhibited. A typical evening meant coming home from school, with dad in his room, grandmother in the kitchen and the smell of dinner greeting you at the door. It would have been nice to have one of them greeting me, but no one seemed to care how my day was. We ate in shifts—the younger first, then my older siblings—but my father ate in his bedroom.

After dinner, we all proceeded to my mother and father's bedroom. My father would position us close to the bed, each of us sitting up straight on the floor to watch television. I never understood what this was all about, but when he would fall asleep, we would sneak out one by one.

There were times when my grandmother finished cleaning the kitchen, and my sisters and I were allowed to go upstairs with her. Going upstairs with my grandmother was a welcomed relief, but there was one rule. We had to be very quiet so as not to disturb my father.

Looking back, I wonder if my father was afraid to be alone, or if he was dealing with some sense of paranoia. As I look back at some of his responses and reactions to certain things, it appeared that my father had suffered from some type of mental health issue stemming from his time in the armed services. I remember my mother saying that my father returned from the services changed, and not for the better. He decided to turn to the bottle to deal with whatever was haunting him. My mother, unfortunately, bore most of the brunt of my father's alcoholic outbursts and emotional physical abuse.

With a family dynamic such as this, I often wondered what my infancy might have been like, considering all the dysfunction. Based on the stories, I often wondered what kind of mother-infant bonding took place during the hospital stay.

I understand that things were a lot different back in the day, and I remember my mother expressed a sigh of relief regarding her hospital stay. Infants spent more time in the nursery, and Mom's hospital stay included bonding time during feedings—but night feedings were done by the nurses in the nursery. My mother said that was the best, because she could sleep, and there were no worries about home as my grandmother was caring for my siblings. It became apparent that my grandmother lived with us to help my mother with child rearing. Now with the birth of twins and me with special needs, my mother needed all the help she could get.

My father's response, as I was told, was one of disappointment, because he was hoping for another boy. *"My goodness, he had four boys already, would another girl be so bad?"* My arrival, unfortunately, was overshadowed with expressions of disappointment.

My home was far from the happy home. It was absent of safety, security, communication, boundaries, and a nourishing environment. A nourishing environment serves as some of the building blocks that leads to a healthy functioning home. I must admit there were times of laughter and play outside or in the playroom downstairs, but it was short-lived. When my father entered the home, there was a cloud of deep silence. Talking turned to whispering, steps were carefully calculated so as not to break the deep silence—all in an effort to stay out of my father's sight.

There were times when my father's actions would fit the profile of what would be described as a tyrant. Some things that took place in the home would be hard for some to believe. As a hunter my father owned guns, which posed a problem when he would go through one of his tirades. He would leave them in plain sight. I assume this was an intimidation tactic, or part of his paranoia.

One afternoon, I went into my mom and dad's room. I don't know why I did it, but I lifted my father's pillow, and there was a hammer. I ran to my grandmother and told her what I saw. My grandmother ignored me and continued to wash dishes. There was no emotion, no sense of urgency.

"Leave it," she said.

Completely perplexed, I left the kitchen—wondering if I should move it. It was just a thought, but I was only a child and there was nothing I could do. This was just one of my father's erratic behaviors—just like the day I had gone shopping with my mother, and upon our return, found my father walking around downstairs with a gun in hand.

This type of erratic behavior had become all too common.

It was not until years later that I had the opportunity of learning my father's narrative. I can empathize with his actions, not excuse them, but gain understanding as to why he acted as such. I had come to realize his tours of duty in the armed services was no joke.

I remember my father shared that as a soldier, you never made friends, because you never knew whether you would see them the next day. Some of his war stories did not make much sense to me, and I often wondered why my father sacrificed so much in the armed services that was overshadowed with unfair treatment and racism to people of color. I can only imagine coming home was no picnic either, after living through that type of experience. I do not know what my father endured during his two tours of duty, but it was enough for him to crawl to the bottle to deal with the torments of the Armed Services.

My real struggle in recollecting childhood memories also includes my mother. It was like she would appear, then disappear. My mother worked nights and my father worked days, and looking back I can see why my mother worked opposite of my father. It was not for childcare reasons, for my maternal grandmother lived with us and did the cooking and cleaning, in addition to getting us ready for school when we were younger. I remember getting ready for school, my energy barely concealed. Grandma would frown.

"Hush girl, you know Ma is sleeping," she'd say.

It was years later that I learned my mother's habit of working nights was a break away from my father.

One summer when I was eight years old, I remember sitting in the front yard. I heard my father raise his voice, and then came a loud noise that sounded like a rubber band being snapped. I remember looking toward the front door of the house and seeing my mother come out of the house, rubbing her cheek.

I can still close my eyes and see my mother rubbing her cheek like it was yesterday. My father came out behind my mother, apologizing and making an excuse as to why he slapped her.

I sat frozen, never taking my eyes off my mother rubbing her cheek. They both went back into the house. I am not even sure if they realized that I was sitting there witnessing the entire ordeal.

For the rest of the day, I was afraid. From that day forward I feared my father and avoided him as much as possible.

My father could have been the poster boy for what is described as an authoritarian father. My father was extremely strict, punitive, controlling, and demanding. We were raised under the premise that children were seen and not heard, thoughts and feelings were never expressed, and there was no room for negotiation.

As for me, I was invisible. There was no emotional connection to my father, and in no way was I "Daddy's little girl." I do not recollect any conversations with my mother until I was at least a young adult after graduating from high school. I did come to learn that my mother's affections were directed exclusively toward her sons.

Unfortunately, what I had witnessed that summer day was just the beginning of many such episodes of verbal and physical abuses that plagued my family home. As the violence increased, there were calls to the police department, who would show up and talk to my father. They would encourage my father to take a walk to calm down and instruct my mother when he gets "like this" to take a ride. It was so embarrassing, having recently moved to a nice quiet neighborhood, to have police constantly showing up at our house. But when they showed up, they did nothing.

All too quickly, the abuse ran rampant in my household. The verbal and physical abuse was no longer restricted to my mother—even my maternal grandmother experienced the physical abuse of my father.

As I grew older, my father distanced himself from my sisters and me. There were many times when my father would have his friends over, and my sisters and I were instructed to go upstairs in my grandmother's room and stay very quiet. My father seemed to take pride in his sons and to regret bringing girls into his world, for we were rarely introduced when company came to visit.

I remember quite clearly my parents hosting a huge barbecue, with friends and family and my brothers in attendance. Unfortunately, my sisters and I viewed the festivities via an upstairs bedroom window. It must have been summertime, maybe Memorial Day, because it was so hot. We spent most of the time upstairs in the closet, and I never understood why. In hindsight, it could be that the only bathroom was upstairs adjacent to the room we were in, therefore requiring us to remain out of sight. My grandmother brought up hot dogs and Kool-Aid and sat with us as the music and laughter from outside filled the room.

Thanksgiving and Christmas were the biggest and most memorable holidays for my family, fostering good childhood memories. These two holidays were the only times there was a sense of normalcy in the family. I always looked forward to Thanksgiving and especially Christmas, as it was during these times that my father appeared normal. There was no arguing and less tension.

I especially looked forward to Christmas as my paternal aunt would come for Christmas and stay a while. My father was a different person when my aunt would come to visit. I don't know what influence she had over him, but I didn't care—if it brought some sort of normalcy, it was welcomed. At Christmas, we appeared as a well-functioning family, doing what families do, showing love and a peaceful togetherness. When my aunt visited, regardless of the holiday, I would not only receive a number of gifts, but much-needed attention as well.

During the summer months, I was shipped off to my aunt's house to spend a couple of weeks. It was nice for a couple of years, but the novelty soon wore off. As I got older, I was able to see more, and I began to see my aunt in a different light. When she was in her element, she was not that nice aunt that came to visit and saved the day. My aunt was verbally abusive. I would hear how she talked to my uncle, and how she treated my cousin. My aunt was mean, just plain mean. I no longer welcomed those summer visits, and I felt bad for my uncle and my cousin. If I wanted to be in an abusive environment, I could have stayed home.

It was not until well into my young adulthood that the abuse against my mother began to lessen as my father's abusive actions were no longer tolerated. Not only did I get older, but so did my siblings, and his abusive actions were now met with resistance.

I remember coming home from school and my father meeting me in the driveway, which was unheard of. I am sure he saw the confusion on my face as I approached the house. I did not say anything. I was intent on getting into the house, as fear began to grip me with a huge sense of uncertainty. For I had experienced my father's mood swings all too often, where he seemed nice for a moment, then would quickly turn into this monster, and I wanted no part of it.

My father stopped me with, "I'm leaving, you will not see me anymore."

I had no reaction. I was left with a thought of "*and*"? What was I to say?

"OK," I mustered up.

I had nothing else to offer. My father reached out and hugged me.

"I'll miss everyone," he said.

It was an extremely awkward moment.

With my father out of the house and my life, I assumed life would be easier—that home would now be a safe place. Hope appeared on the horizon. The stillness of peace would be a welcomed addition. Unfortunately, the abuse continued, as the spirit of my father remained. Men continued to rule the roost, as my father had so exemplified. Men were superior, women were low on the totem pole, and I was treated as such.

A major shift occurred, and certainly not for the good.

I was in my senior year in high school when my grandmother became ill, and I assumed some of my grandmother's tasks. I became a slave to the males of the home, doing their laundry and cleaning their rooms. Since my mother continued to work the night shift, I became one of the cooks. Staying out of the house had quickly become a priority, as home remained unsafe—no protection, no support, no encouragement. My dreams of going to college seemed but a distant memory. Confronting my mother about college, I was met with slight annoyance, as she stated there was no money for college. There appeared to be no hope of a future—at least for me, anyway.

A few years later, my thoughts about how my mother felt about women in the family were affirmed when my mom helped my brother to attend college. Again, further affirmation that I must take control of my future and destiny.

But God had a plan.

DREAM, DREAM, AND DREAM

Unfulfilled dreams are goals never achieved.

My grandmother would always talk of the dreams she had, like dreams of having her own home with a nice yard. These dreams were on hold and unfulfilled for she committed herself to helping her youngest daughter, my mom, care for her children. Each time one of my brothers or sisters were old enough, she would make plans to fulfill her dreams.

Eleven grandchildren later, my grandmother was pretty much stuck. Her dreams and desire of a small house on a large piece of land with a nice fence preoccupied many of the stories and dreams she shared, each resonating as a dream deferred. As the author Langston Hughes' poem questions, was her dream dried up like a "raisin in the sun"? Her dreams were never fulfilled, and all her dreams died with her passing away.

My grandmother's living was not all together in vain. As a woman of great faith, she would be happy to know that her prayers and her grooming me into a woman of faith was a dream fulfilled. At an early age, my grandmother began grooming me for such a time as this.

It was under the guidance of my grandmother that I became a woman of God, a preacher, and a teacher of God's word. Out of all my siblings, my grandmother saw fit to share the word of God with me. She would have me read scriptures, specifically the Lord's Prayer from Matthew 6:9-13 and Psalm 121:1-8. These two scriptures were recited in the morning and before I went to bed.

I continued reciting these scriptures after my grandmother's death, and I still recite today. My grandmother would rise at 6:00 am. I would wake up and see her sitting in a chair facing toward the rising sun, reading the Bible and praying softly.

I remember times when my siblings and I were playing (whether indoors or outdoors), and I would be called to my grandmother's room. She would instruct me to sit down, where she would talk with me about God and have me read and recite Matthew 6:9-13 and Psalm 121:1-8. There were times I was somewhat upset, but I dare not show it, not in those days. Why was I the one that had to pray and read the Bible and listen to stories about God? My grandmother must have known something that I would come to understand in due time, but now was not the time.

I was saddened for my grandmother when her illness warranted a move to a nursing home. I never understood why she was placed in a nursing home. She spent her whole life caring for us, so why couldn't we return the favor?

But being in a nursing home did not stop her from sharing her dreams of a better life and a hope for tomorrow. I would visit her often in the nursing home, and as she shared her stories, I would comb her hair and listen intently. I soon began to minister to her, reading Bible verses to her—especially the Book of Psalms—as she had taught me. When the Lord called her home, I became a spiritual orphan. But one thing I did—I continued to read the scriptures and pray, never realizing that preparation for ministry continued.

It was not long after my father had left the home that the oldest male siblings took control. I'm speaking of an abusive nature that was inherited from my father that continued to play out in the family dynamic. The words of my mother still ring in my soul: "Your father is gone, do what you want."

It was like a dog whistle, *do what you want,* words taken literally. The family environment remained toxic and lacked any sense of boundaries, leaving me emotionally and physically vulnerable. My grandmother taught me how to dream, now I dreamed of a place far, far away.

My mom had always relied on the older male siblings for protection from my father, but once my father was out of the home, who was going to protect me from them? I quickly learned that no one would protect you, so you have to learn to protect yourself physically, emotionally and psychologically. How was I to do this? I had far from perfect parenting. One of the attributes of parenting is to provide safety, supervision, and protection from harm—none of which I experienced in my family of origin.

Living in an abusive environment precipitated the need to vicariously live through television families, and this was as close that I could get to a "normal family." Shows like "Father Knows Best," "The Brady Bunch," and "The Partridge Family" provided a temporary escape, but also a misconception that this type of family dynamic did not consist within families of color. When a family of color did come on the scene, they lived in the ghetto of Chicago with dreams of one day getting out. Thank God for The Cosby's and the Jeffersons; I guess dreams can come true.

To gain control over my life, I made a vow to never be like my mother. A submissive woman with no "voice." I definitely never wanted to be the controlling, domineering tyrant that my father was.

Shortly after graduation, I moved out of my home in hopes of gaining not only independence but getting control of my life. But unfortunately, I brought every ounce of dysfunction with me. I found myself in relationships playing second fiddle or relationships that were just as abusive as the environment I was running from. Coming up in a family of dysfunction and being an adult child of an alcoholic (ACOA), what else could I expect but to end up being second fiddle and in abusive relationships.

I tolerated these relationships because I felt I did not deserve better, and actually, that's all I had come to know. It's ironic that I gravitated to the very thing I hated and despised. When I finally came to realize that I deserved to be treated as number one, and I met the abuse with fighting back, these relationships quickly dissolved. I felt proud of myself, finally taking a stand against being disrespected, devalued, and abused.

It was at this liberating moment that I met my husband, but not without some residual baggage. I entered this relationship, which led to marriage—confident as a woman who could hold her own, especially as I had given my heart to the Lord and become a woman of faith. I now had a voice and took control of every aspect of my life.

Little did I know that everything that comes with being a victim of physical and verbal abuse and an ACOA remained deeply imbedded and untouched, masked with strict religiosity. All this untouched baggage was brought into my marriage, which almost led to its demise. During my marriage I was controlling and domineering. It was my way or no way, since I was the "religious one." As my marriage was in jeopardy, I came to realize that in an effort to not become my mother, I had become the very one that I hated: my father.

As a new convert in Christ, I found myself with quite a few questions regarding Christianity. Although my grandmother had me praying and reciting scriptures at a young age, that did not mean I had surrendered my life to Christ. Long after my grandmother had passed away, I still found myself reciting the scriptures, the Lord's Prayer from Matthew 6:9-13, and Psalm 121, especially in times of trouble. I had come to a place desiring to know more of the personhood of God. If God protects those who are His, if He heals, saves, and rescues, what kind of God allows His child to be subjected to an environment of abuse?

Reflecting on my grandmother's life, I often wondered how she managed to keep the faith while living in such a dysfunctional environment. She was able to continue to dream of a better life. I came to an understanding that there had to be more to this walk than just reciting scriptures and attending Sunday service at my local church. I signed up to participate in the Bible study classes hoping to build a foundation for further learning and spiritual development.

I wanted to get to know this God that my grandmother held so dear. I continued to study God's word, I became intrigued with the nature of God, His relationship with humanity, and humanity's need for a Savior, Jesus Christ. With a desire for Christianity to be a lifestyle and not just a formalized religion, I enrolled in Bible school, and from Bible school into seminary. This was all to further my quest of not only studying God's word, but also growing closer to Him.

This journey not only served as a learning journey, but also as a healing journey as well. It gave me the opportunity to work through the pain of my past. Attending seminary prepared me for ministry and counseling, and it became a useful tool for me as I began to minister outside the walls of the church.

It was through my course work in seminary that I invested in becoming a pastoral counselor. My course work in seminary and pastoral counseling not only offered a solid foundation in theology and spirituality, but also in psychology. These building blocks of biblical principles, concepts of psychology and psychotherapy, served as a solid platform for ministry and servitude.

These building blocks also opened doors for an internship as a volunteer chaplain. Serving as a volunteer chaplain at the local sheriff's department, I discovered many of the inmates that came to the Sunday morning worship services were not only broken in spirit and soul, but also had lost hope. Most presented with anger, frustration, and depression. Those suffering from anxiety also presented with family of origin issues. The enhanced training that I received in pastoral counseling equipped me with the tools that were needed to address the many issues presented by the inmates.

I continued my internship and ministry within the sheriff's department and within the church sector. As I continued to minister to my fellow congregates, it was of little surprise that most presented with trauma stemming from unresolved childhood and family issues.

I saw the need to further my education in meeting the psychological needs of not just the inmates, but also the individuals within the church sector. It quickly became apparent that there was an increased benefit of treating within the context of relationships.

My grandmother's dreams were not only of a home with a picket fence, and a better life, but a dream of a person to continue to pray and cover the family with God's word. My grandmother passed that dream of a better life that comes through Christ to her granddaughter, *me.*

PEACE IN THE
MIDST OF IT ALL

The abused children are alone with their suffering not only
Within the family, but also within themselves.
They cannot share their pain with anyone.
They cannot create a place in their own soul where
They could cry their heart out.
Alice Miller

Growing up in my family, females quickly learned their place within the family dynamic. Some of the overt messages was that of complete submission, never usurping the authority of the men of the house. Anything other than submission was viewed as being headstrong, domineering, or masculine. Women were to be submissive, caring for children and the household. The women of my family were in charge of making sure dinner was on the table, laundry was done, and the house was clean. Gender roles in our family meant women did all the housework and even the yard work.

During my graduate studies in marriage and family therapy, I created a genogram of three generations of my family of origin. A genogram is a family diagram used to capture the relationships between family members. It also spots behavioral patterns across multiple generations. An *overt* message of my family of origin was that of "keep them barefoot and pregnant." By keeping the women bearing children, you will keep them under your thumb, because who else would want you with all those children?

It's this type of antiquated thinking that kept my mother in the maternity ward. I remember my mother telling me that she got married at an early age because during those times women had little opportunities, my father was going into the service, and she had nothing else to do.

A *covert* message within my family dynamic was that men were superior to women. If the male siblings did well in school and got good grades, there was much praise and celebration. But for my accomplishments, such as good grades, there was very little fanfare, even though I got much better grades. This left me with feelings of inadequacy and a sense of never being able to measure up to my male siblings. When conducting interviews for my genealogy, it showcased males playing an abusive role in their marriages. They used abuse, whether emotional, verbal, or physical to "keep their wives in line."

Both paternal and maternal grandmothers performed domestic duties in the home and outside of the home. Both grandmothers were very submissive and subservient to their husbands in spite of the abuse. There was certainly a double standard as they were very strict with their daughters and lenient with their son(s).

I remember challenging my mother on the double standard in which I was raised, and she replied that "boys were not the ones that would bring home a baby, but girls will." I didn't even bother to challenge this antiquated ideology. I assumed it was okay for the boys to go out and have babies everywhere, just as long they did not bring them home. These so-called girls were someone else's daughters which would be bringing home a baby.

I guess this antiquated reasoning resonated throughout my family history, as among the males there were multiple marriages and outside relationships that yielded children, further solidifying that it's okay for males to "sow their wild oats," as this was part of being masculine. To show one's masculinity was to be domineering, controlling, and authoritative, which my father so exemplified—so my male siblings followed suit.

Being submissive and quiet was part of being feminine, and any type of assertiveness was quickly met by verbal and physical repercussions. As a female being seen and not heard was definitely the rule within my household growing up. The script in which I became loyal to was one of "women were created for man's pleasure; we were not our own."

Growing up as a female adolescent, there were no sex talks or sex education within my home. To speak of sex was a taboo topic. As a young girl broaching womanhood, there were no conversations about puberty or hormonal changes that a young girl would experience. I was what they called a "late bloomer." I did not begin menstruation until my late teens, 19 years of age to be exact. What I learned, I learned from my sisters' experiences.

I would overhear my grandmother instructing my sisters on how to maintain cleanliness during their cycles. Even when instructions were given, words like "vagina" were never referenced. She would say "make sure you keep that thing clean" or another word was "porcupine." I was always reluctant to ask questions about sexuality, sexual orientation, or the changes that were happening within my body. Any question that remotely touched on the subject was met with resistance and almost rebuke. The response was always, "Why are you asking those type of questions?"—implying I was up to something.

My family of origin also consisted of affairs, divorces, remarriages, and secrets. Sex brought guilt, shame, and denial. Female sexuality seemed to only bring embarrassment to the family. There were teen pregnancies, abortions, and procedures done to prevent promiscuity. Most of what I learned relative to sex education was from peers. My mother never talked about sex with me; I never got "the talk."

I remember going out on my first date. As I was walking out the door, my mother spoke.

"Keep your legs closed and your skirt down," she said.

"I'm not wearing a skirt, I'm wearing pants," I replied.

She was not happy with my response. The sex talk was limited to "if you are going to engage in sexual activity, get on the pill."

Femininity had overtones of oppression which equated to trouble. Femininity brought with it negative connotations, and any expression of one's sensual side was shameful. Living in an abusive environment, I did not desire to be in touch with my feminine side as it only brought misery. Any attempt, if at all, only served to elicit guilt and shame, as it opened the door to physical and sexual abuse. I grew to curse my femininity and developed a distain of anything sexual.

For some, coming into womanhood would be a time of joy, as femininity is part of one's inner beauty. For me it was a time of sadness rather than joy. Menstruation was referred to as the "curse" and it certainly felt like it. My grandmother had strong beliefs relative to menstruation. For her anyone who was on their menstruation was "unclean" (right out of the Old Testament). While you were on your "cycle," you could not cook or water her plants. She believed that if you touched them, they would die. My grandmother could be described as a strict legalistic Pentecostal who took the word of God literally. Again, leaving me with feelings of being cursed, dirty, and undesirable.

A review of my family genogram further revealed that there was little to no intimacy and sex seemed to be a dutiful act. It was the wife's duty to submit unto her husband. Sex was just another task, like taking out the garbage or doing laundry.

Physical and sexual abuse was prevalent in my family of origin through three generations, which includes this current generation. For my generation, the response to the ongoing sexual abuse was, "You aren't pregnant, are you?" or "Just say no." The sense of worthlessness, not worthy of defending, and being at fault was the prevailing attitude within this conflict avoidant atmosphere. This negative script prevailed throughout my life right into my marriage.

A disengaged father, emotionally distant mother, no boundaries, and a grandmother strong in her legalistic Pentecostal faith, is counterproductive to a child's emotional and psychological development. Based on my family genogram, these behavioral patterns were sadly across multiple generations.

Things were no better when my father left. I lived in fear and hyper-sensitivity to my environment, scanning every room prior to entering. The bathroom and the closets served as gate ways to darkness; never knowing what or who lies within the shadows. For many years, well into my adulthood, I would find myself checking and scanning. Whether at a friend's house or hotels, I proceeded with caution and anxiety.

Physical abuse also came by way of the stairs, I say to myself, *but why*, what enjoyment came out of grabbing me by the ankles and dragging me down the stairs, causing bruising and pain to my chest, rug burns on my arms, and broken nails as I attempted to grip the carpet on the stairs to release myself from this dysfunction. I began wearing clothing that appeared uninviting to ward off unwanted touch and inappropriate stares.

I constantly asked myself, *why was this happening to me, why would someone who should be looking out for me and protecting me violate me this way? You are the one who should be telling me to look out for guys like you. Home is to be a safe place. When the streets are unsafe, home should be a place of refuge, where I can be protected and sheltered from the perils of the streets. Where am I to turn, no place is safe, no one can be trusted.*

I began to be watchful and vigilant. What's around the corner, what waits behind the door? I struggled not to slip into darkness. Fear would paralyze my very being, I went into my corner and looked to the sky. That was my secret corner, it was my place of escape. In the eye of any storm is peace. I would allow myself to slip into that place where the skies were blue, the sun shined, and the white pillowy clouds became a welcoming escape. I would find myself surrounded by sunlight, embracing its warmth and comfort. Blue skies and white clouds seemed to break through the darkness that attempted to encapsulate me.

I embraced it all with welcoming arms. My thoughts were racing, I assured myself that I could rest here for a moment. It may be over for now, but I needed to strategize a way of not getting caught the next time. I was unfortunately in the wrong place at the wrong time—how stupid of me. I must be more vigilant and mindful of my surroundings. Nowhere is safe. I had no one to turn to and no place to go.

My very being was filled with anger—I was angry towards my mom for not protecting me, angry at them for hating me so much to warrant this type of violation, and angry at God for allowing this to happen. All that my grandmother had taught me about God's love and protection and prayer seemed like a fable. The sad thing is that I hated my body because it was mostly at fault. I never considered myself as being a beauty queen, I definitely did not have the figure "8" body. Maybe I was so undesirable that they figured I would welcome any attention.

For a long time, my body was not my friend. It betrayed me on several occasions. I disowned it, as it no longer belonged to me anyway. It took time—a long time—for me to forgive and to love my body again. I have come to realize the shadows of the past do not have to be the reality of my future.

Any form of sexual abuse has negative long-term effects for the victim, especially when the abuser is a family member. Incestuous abuse destroys the very foundation of what it is to be family: trust and safety. This type of abuse stripped away any sense of safety and stability.

The National Center for Biotechnology Information states some of the symptoms of sexual abuse are headaches, sadness, irritability, and anger, to name a few. Research shows that sexual and physical abuse coupled with emotional instability are associated with increased risk of GERD and Acid Reflux. I suffered with these symptoms for years, never having a full understanding of the root cause. I remember attending social and family functions experiencing knots in my stomach so bad that I could not eat or if I ate, I would have to excuse myself as I struggled to keep food down.

These egregious experiences created a negative frame of reference when it came to sexuality and my sense of self. My childhood maltreatment resonated a perceived lack of social support, which led to poor self-esteem and living in fear. This type of fear leaves one powerless, and wounds create barriers. I struggled with feelings of insecurity, and certainly had serious trust issues. Anger is the feeling that resonated with me for years. It only masked the deep-seated pain and frustration that dwelled within. Questions upon questions kept me up at night and served as a distraction during the day. The biggest question of all was, *why didn't my mother protect me, who wouldn't protect their little girl? Why were my needs placed second to my male siblings? Did anyone care?* For me, the answer was clearly *no.*

The emotional and sexual abuse led to a lack of understanding of how a healthy relationship(s) work. I had no standard to compare with, and dysfunction is all I knew. The few relationships that I experienced were abusive and emotionally taxing. These relationships were filled with unrealistic expectations and hope. There was a constant yearning for the care and support that came with any healthy relationship, whatever that looked like. In hindsight I tended to gravitate toward what was familiar, and that is dysfunction. I settled for these relationships, believing I was not deserving of a healthy, caring relationship, or to even be treated with respect. Here I was, feeling trapped in abusive relationships with no way of escape. The more I tried to pull away, the worst it got. I would hear the same old lines that I would hear my father say to my mother after one of his abusive acts: "Sorry I didn't mean it, you made me mad," like I had that much power over their emotions.

Everyone has a breaking point, and I was no different.

I remember like it was yesterday.

I went to my ex's mother's house to pick up some personal items that I had left at their house. When I arrived, she let me in, and I told her that I was there just to pick up my things. She knew that we had been broken up for some weeks. My ex was there, but he didn't say anything to me, and I said nothing to him. His mom was on her way out the door for work, and I finished gathering my things and was leaving right behind her, when I was stopped at the door. He had that same look in his eye when he got angry. He was shaking his head, mumbling under his breath. I asked him to move, as I heard the outside apartment door close, letting me know that his mother had left.

Then it started. He grabbed me by my arm and shoved me back into the apartment. Things began to get foggy. *Here it goes again.* I remember pushing him away, fighting to get him away from me. He dragged me down the hallway toward the bedroom, and all the while I was kicking, scratching, and screaming. I was blanking out. He was hurting me.

At this moment, it was like a switch came on, things got foggy, I don't remember everything, there was this silence. What I do remember is that before I realized it, I had an empty wine bottle in my hand. I broke it against the wall and went for him. There was a loud knock at the door that brought me back. I stood frozen, my heart racing, I was shaking all over.

My ex ran from the room to answer the door. It was the police. Someone must have heard the screaming. I heard my ex telling the police that I was trying to stab him. One of the officers came to me, asking if I was okay. I dropped the broken bottle and said I wanted to leave.

The officer walked me outside, asked if I wanted to file a complaint. I told him no, I just wanted to go home. I got in my car, still shaking, and drove home, thinking I almost seriously hurt someone, possibly killing him. At that time, it was either him or me.

When I arrived home, no one was home, thank God. I went to the bathroom, and looking in the mirror, I saw I had slight red bruising on my face, and my arms and shoulders had welts obviously from the struggle. I assume that is why the officer asked if I wanted to file a complaint. I stared in the mirror, I don't know how long, trying to figure out who this person was in the mirror. I looked at the welts. I remember rubbing them, and realizing these welts did not just tell the story of the here and now, but a deeper narrative, one of manipulation and abuse manifesting into rage.

Lord, I need help.

This negative frame of reference carried well into my marriage. My husband is a very affectionate man, but for me I didn't want to appear affectionate or take the risk of being intimate. I was not sure if I knew how. When my husband showed affection, I thought it was a sign for wanting sex, so being the dutiful wife, I would submit to his advances, even when I did not want to. One day my husband wanted to cuddle, and I assumed it was time for sex.

He pulled away from me and asked, "Why does everything have to end with sex with you, can't we just hold each other?"

As far as initiating, that was never my role, mostly for fear of being labeled. I did not want my husband to think that I was "fast"; I wanted him to see me as innocent, not damaged goods.

Along with this came the feelings of embarrassment relative to my body image. I never felt attractive, must less sexy. This would annoy my husband a lot. No matter how often he complimented me, I just could not receive it. I could not accept my femininity so how could I expect my husband to? My husband was offering everything that I lacked in my childhood, nurturance, acceptance, and genuine love. It was hard for me to receive this from my husband; this was a strange area for me. There were times when we were intimate, and I felt myself just going through the motions just to satisfy him.

My sexual abuse only served to stifle my vulnerability. Vulnerability is a sacrifice of comfort, allowing yourself to be potential prey to emotional abuse. True intimacy warrants vulnerability. It is sharing our innermost selves with another loving, safe soul that we trust, and it is the deepest connection. Vulnerability allows us to be our authentic selves, but past emotional abuse can make it hard to trust.

Chronic emotional abuse can affect how you see yourself in relationships and your tolerance toward certain behaviors. I carried around ingrained scripts of negativity from my family of origin. Here I was being loyal to my family legacy. It is hard to enjoy intimacy when saluting shameful legacies at the same time. Legacies such as sacrificing my own feelings in order to please another; just as long as the other person is satisfied; sex is for men; women are to submit.

My past abuse was the huge elephant in my marriage. It was a secret that I just could not share with my husband. Initially, I was so afraid that he would not look at me the same; he would see me as dirty with a lack of innocence. This silence only served to intensify the shame that I carried.

It was in therapy that I was able to process the dysfunctionality and the abuse that I endured. Was it easy? Absolutely not. It often took me to dark places, the places that I had locked the door on a long time ago. I did find it freeing and refreshing that I could speak about this part of my personhood. But I was not able to share the spiritual aspect, the brokenness of my spirit and soul, and the grappling with the question, where was God? This part of my being, only God could answer. I looked to God and He answered me.

I had a dream of my spirit floating through the air, surrounded by darkness. As I was floating, my heart was racing, and fear gripped me as I turned down a street. There was something familiar about this street. There was an eerie silence, and a deep darkness covered the landscape. I felt myself approaching something, but I could not make out what it was. My heart rate increased even more. Then there it was: my childhood house.

Notice I say "house," as it was never a home. Here is where it all happened. Shrouded in darkness, I awoke sweating and shaking. I called on the name of Jesus, I gathered myself, and lied back down, afraid to fall back to sleep.

I had this dream twice, and realized I must go to that dark place that was under lock and key. I needed to release it and allow God to heal the inner most part of my being. It is only now that I realized that I needed to go to that dark place and heal. Because there will come a time when I would need to go to the dark places of my client's soul and minister the light of Jesus. I cannot take anyone anywhere that I have not gone myself. For this, I am eternally grateful to God.

I thank God for affording me the opportunity to participate in seminary and education in marriage and family therapy, as it provided the space to process and reconcile both my physical and spiritual being. I stopped focusing on the whys and began to focus on the where, meaning where I was in my healing journey. I can safely say that I was moving to a place of freedom from the bondage that plagued my life. I utilized the tools that therapy had to offer in relieving the anxiety and low self-worth, but it was the integrating of both psychotherapy and the disciplines of spirituality that promoted the healing of my whole person.

GRIEF HAS NO RESPECT OF PERSON

I t was a special day for my son, we were sitting in the closing office, as he was about to close on his condo.

As I sat next to him waiting for his attorney and real-estate agent, I let my son know how proud I was of him becoming a homeowner. I felt honored to support him in this huge milestone in his life. We both worked hard to get him to this moment.

My son turns to me and asks, "Are you alright?"

He was checking in with me because that morning I had received the phone call that my mother was transitioning; she was losing her battle with pancreatic cancer. I let my son know that I was okay, as we knew six months ago that this was a battle that she would not win.

A few months prior, I took the trip to the south to see my mother after I got the call that my mom was admitted to the hospital. She was experiencing severe stomach issues, which she shared she had been experiencing for weeks.

* * *

When I arrived, my sister picked me up from the airport. I asked her what was happening with mom. My sister said that our mom had been sick for some time, she just didn't let anyone know. My heart started to sink, and I felt a tightness in my chest.

My God, what if my mother dies? Why now? We were on the road toward reconciliation, and I was now able to visit often without the knot in my stomach. We had plans to have that mother-daughter relationship that I had always prayed for.

It was two years ago that I flew down to speak with my mother and to ask for her forgiveness for the anger that I held against her for years. With a knot in my stomach, I shared my disappointments and how the abuse had played out in my life. The more I shared, the more the knot in my stomach loosened. I was careful when I shared, as I was concerned about hurting my mother's feelings. She had been beaten down enough.

My mom moved south to escape the high taxes as most seniors do, but I always thought it was more than the high taxes. But since she moved south, it was not all that she hoped it to be. She once told me that she missed New York.

My mother was a wounded, vulnerable woman, non-confrontational, always with a flight response. I was careful not to be harsh, for the woman that sat before me was a broken woman, riddled with guilt. Mom was still harboring the symptoms of persistent emotional and physical abuse. Coming down on her would serve no purpose.

I apologized to my mom for being angry and harboring this resentment towards her. My mom acknowledged the anger that I had towards her, and said she knew it for some time.

With her head down, my mom responded, "I'm so sorry."

She never looked at me but continued to look down. It was like she was looking back over her life.

I felt ashamed for harboring this anger for so long. Hers was a narrative saturated with unfulfilled dreams and regrets and fear.

"I am so sorry, please forgive me, Mom," I said.

"No, I apologize, forgive me," she said.

My perception and feelings toward my mother changed at that moment. Her narrative moved me to a place of empathy and pity. That day, I saw my mother in a different light. She was not a woman who didn't care for her little girl. She was a woman who could not protect herself, distancing from her daughter so as not to feel a mother's pain for their child; gravitating to her sons in hopes one day they would rescue her.

* * *

My thoughts were interrupted by the para legal assisting with the closing, and my son and I entered the conference room. With a sense of pride, I entered with my son, as he had took a step closer to becoming a responsible adult.

As I watched, I began reflecting on how much he had matured into a fine young man. It was not an easy road getting here, but he did it. We had worked for a year in cleaning up his credit and settling outstanding debt.

I checked my cell phone for the time. It was 11:30 a.m.—30 minutes since we started the closing process. I still hadn't received any additional news from my sister. My mind continued to drift in and out of the closing process. I needed to get to Georgia as soon as possible. I continued to tell myself that this could not be happening.

* * *

When I left Georgia two months ago, after helping my sister with mom, I promised her that I would be back to spend her birthday with her. The morning of my flight to New York, I went to her room. She was lying in bed, listening to Christian music. As I leaned over to give her a kiss on the forehead, she opened her eyes.

I told her that it was time for me to go, and she took my hand. Her hand was light as a feather, she looked me in the eye. Her eyes drooped with weakness, and there was a deep sadness in her eyes. If eyes are the window to the soul, my mother's soul was steeped in pain and regret.

"Don't go, please stay," she begged me.

My heart sank in my chest and tears came to my eyes. I couldn't stay. I had to get back home to my family and back to work. It was hard letting go of my mother's hand, and as I slowly pulled my hand away, I could feel my mother's soft grip. It was weak, not the hand of a strong woman, but the hand of surrender. This was a battle that my mom was not going to win. Each time I recall that moment, I feel it in my heart.

It was a quiet ride to the airport that morning. I guess both my sister and I were locked in our individual thoughts. Arriving at the airport, I gave my sister a hug and told her I would be back to give her a much-needed break from taking care of mom. I guess there is an advantage to having a large family. Each one of my siblings took turns going to our mother's bedside, assisting in caring for her.

Prior to going to my gate, I stopped in the ladies' room to cry as I began to feel a flood of emotions. I did not want to break down in the hallway, so I quickly went into a stall and had a good cry, a cry that was not forced, a cry that came from the deepest part of my soul.

I thank God I had a window seat. I looked out the window the entire time as I didn't want anyone to see the tears that continued to flow down my cheeks.

"I will be back, Mom. Don't worry, I will be back," I whispered to myself.

* * *

The closing was near completion when my sister called me. I had let the attorney know in advance of my situation, so I excused myself to take the call. My heart was beating so hard as I answered. It was my sister, telling me that she was instructed to call the family as my mother did not have much time left, stating that she would not make it through the night. I let her know that I was in closing and would call her back immediately after.

I took a moment to gather myself before going back to the closing office. When I entered the closing room, the closing was complete.

The attendees were shaking my son's hand, congratulating him on becoming a first-time homeowner.

I gave him a hug.

"We have to go, Grandma is leaving us," I whispered.

Four years earlier, I was in Georgia to lay my father to rest, and now I must lay my mother to rest. My mother had suffered so much in the last six months of her life as pancreatic cancer robbed her of life.

This trip back to Georgia was a deeply painful one as I reflected on my mom's suffering. It came with typical family drama, as people's true colors always come to the forefront in times of bereavement.

Frustration began to overtake me as I wrestled with my own inner dialogue.

Why are you crying? I better not see you shed one tear. You are not going to use this time to alleviate your selfish guilt. You have no right to cry. Why are you portraying to be hurt? You have no right to cry. You took advantage of a broken woman. There were red flags all pointing to your manipulation, signs of preying on an elderly woman's vulnerability. Why couldn't she confront you or say no? She could not because she was a victim of her circumstances. Your bullying and intimidation were your chief tactics to get what you wanted.

On her dying bed, you only thought of yourself. Greed dictated your actions. Your actions sadden my heart. She wouldn't allow me to come to her defense for fear of retaliation. I see the books, the ledgers. Your actions, come to think of it, border on financial exploitation. You say those are strong words, but I call it as I see it. May God have mercy upon your soul(s).

A TIME TO MOURN AGAIN

It is the one-year anniversary of my mother's death. I had lost my father a few years earlier. Now I must endure the pain of losing my mother again.

* * *

As I reflected, I remember that prior to my father's death, I had begun to reach out to my father—which was initiated by an argument regarding my mother. I called him because he would call my mother with nonsense and bullying her. I thought, *Really, after all these years you are still acting like a bully?*

I let my father know that day to stop with the nonsense because no one was afraid of him anymore. I told my father that none of us have to call him, much less speak to him. He started to get defensive, but I cut him off, letting him know that he needed us more than we needed him.

It must have been 30 minutes after we had ended the conversation that my mother called. She told me that I had upset my father, and he could not believe that I spoke to him that way. His conversations softened toward my mom and our conversations were much better from that day forward.

I would call my father once per week, every Father's Day, and on his birthday. It would seem ironic that things had changed, considering how abusive and mean my father was. I had vowed never to give this man the time of day, and here I was, calling him and having conversations with him. Like I said, it is not until we learn a person's story that we can move to empathy and forgiveness. I resigned to the fact that there was nothing I could do to change the past, but I could look forward to a better future.

One summer, I made plans to go to Georgia for a short vacation. In speaking with my father, he asked when I would be arriving. I let him know my plans and asked him why he asked. My father shared that he wanted to talk with me. It was ironic.

"When is the Rev coming?" he had asked my sister. (That is how my father addressed me and referred to me.)

It was a hot summer day in Georgia, and we were on the front porch, enjoying the summer sun and warm breezes that the south offered on days like this.

Then it happened—something that neither did I expect nor ever dream of. My father apologized to me.

He shared that he caused the family so much pain, and he asked for forgiveness. I asked him if he had made his peace with God, and he replied with a "Yes." He told me he asked God for forgiveness for his wrongdoing.

I sat in awe, as I never heard my father humble himself and show any sensitivity. This was a man that ruled with an iron fist and had no relationship with me as a little girl, until a few years prior where I took the initiative to foster some sort of relationship.

The whole time he was speaking, he continued to look up towards the sky, and sometimes scanned the landscape. He told me how proud he was when I became an ordained Minister. Sitting next to him was different, and I felt no anxiety or fear—something that I was not accustomed to.

There was like a peace about him, a sense of calm, not that hostile spirit that we were all familiar with. As a matter of fact, he said he had made his peace. I could sense the difference. There was no more fight in him.

My father passed three months after this visit. I got the call from my sister at 1:00 a.m. I reflected on our visit, and how vulnerable my father was. It was nice talking with him, it was nice to see a different side of him. It was also sad, but I didn't focus on the past, but on the future.

It's never too late to reconcile. I was glad that I made the trip to Georgia and spent that week together. I saw him as who he was, not what he had become because of childhood trauma, two tours of duty, and alcoholism.

I remember journaling about my father's passing, writing about how there would be no more phone calls to wish him a happy birthday, Father's Day, or just to see how he was doing.

Some may ask, "After all that your father did, how can you give him the time of day?"

Yes, my father was abusive. I remember having to go to the hospital for pneumonia and while waiting on the couch, my father approached me, stuck his hand out and I remember cringing riddled with fear, trying to brace for the slap. The slap never came. Instead, he was touching my forehead, checking for fever.

I'm saddened by the loss of my father, but more so for missed opportunities; that father-daughter relationship that I desired as a child will never be. The flight home was overshadowed with grief. As the plane took off, I looked out the window and said my final good-bye to my father. Next year would be different, and every year thereafter, I would never see or speak to him again.

* * *

The days leading up to the one-year anniversary of my mother's death were filled with much sadness, wondering if I could make it through the day. As I sat in church one Sunday, I found my thoughts drifting in and out of the service. Listening to the preacher—one moment attentive to his words, another moment getting lost in thoughts of the past.

Thinking about my mother's passing brought forth mixed emotions. Part of me still felt some anger, anger that we were on the path to healing this mother-daughter relationship then she died. Another part was a deep sadness of the missed opportunities to finish some of the unresolved childhood issues.

Some may say, "Why talk about childhood issues? You are an adult now." If I may say so, most of us are adults with a lot of unresolved childhood issues.

I came back to the service for a moment, as a woman on the left side of the church was sharing her testimony of how God healed her of cancer. The members began to praise God and celebrate her healing. I could not share in the celebration, and my heart became heavy. A deep sadness came over me as the entire church rejoiced.

The Scripture says, *Rejoice with those who rejoice; weep with those who weep* (Romans 12:15, KJV). As the church rejoiced, I sat wondering; did it enter anyone's mind that I was in mourning, that I had just gotten back from laying my mother to rest? *Why isn't anyone weeping with me? I know that God can heal, her testimony was a witness to that, why didn't God heal my mother?*

I put my head down and cried softly. Then I felt a gentle touch on my shoulder.

The sister behind me whispered, "It's okay."

She rubbed my shoulder, praying for my comfort and strength. I drifted off again into my thoughts. It was not fair for my mother to pass away, I still had so much more to say, so much more to work through.

* * *

I reflected on my previous visit to see my mother. It was time to release this burden of unforgiveness and apologize to my mom. I reflected on the moment of release and forgiveness and my mother's story. It was a story of sadness, broken dreams and aspirations, emotional and physical abuse, and of never having a voice.

My mother was a survivor. She had beat the odds on several occasions. She survived domestic violence, cancer, a poisonous snake, and the Great Depression. She outlived all her siblings and raised eleven children the best she knew how.

A strong woman some may say, but sitting before me at that moment was a broken woman, with shattered dreams and a shattered disposition. My mother was filled with regrets and secrets—some of which she took to the grave—but her second diagnosis of cancer was one that she could not hide as she did the first.

Another secret that did not go to the grave was her disappointment of having girls. Maybe not so much disappointment, but sadness. As a victim of abuse, my mother could not protect herself, so how was she to protect her little girls?

The years of abuse from my father had taken a serious emotional toll on my mother. Long after her separation from my father, my mother was a woman bound by her past, a past that forever kept her a prisoner mentally and psychologically. I watched my mother's behavior and reactions around my older brothers. It was one of submission, non-confrontation, and silence. I thought to myself, *Dad is long gone, where is your voice? You have a voice for your girls, but not your boys.* It would make me angry to hear and see how they would speak to my mother. It triggered something in me and reminded me of my father.

My last words to my mom were via phone. The nurse instructed my sister that it was time to notify the family that my mother was transitioning. My sister called me, and I asked my sister to put the phone to my mother's ear.

I said a prayer for my mother and let her know that I loved her, that it was her time to rest in the arms of Jesus.

My mother let out a soft groan and passed away.

My thoughts drifted back to the service, and I quickly wiped my face as I realized that tears were running down my cheeks. I checked my watch. It was 5:45 p.m., the time that my mother took her last breath. Still, I grieve.

* * *

As a pastoral counselor and marriage and family therapist, grief is a word that I have come to know all too well. I am called upon to aide others in their loss, whether through loss of a job, divorce, familial conflict, or tragedy. How does one grieve when others look to you for emotional support and comfort? You are supposed to be strong; you are the counselor—a pastoral counselor, at that. We are perceived to have a special relationship with God; therefore, we are a pillar of strength. With a heart of compassion, our faith is attributed to our resilience.

As pastoral counselors, we are called to walk alongside those that grieve, equipped with the tools to minister and counsel those in bereavement.

But what about me? As a pastoral counselor, with whom do I share my pain and brokenness? I am expected to be strong for the family, clients, peers; to pray, to support and console. Do I dare allow myself to be vulnerable, to shift from a role of pastoral counselor to a grieving individual? I am to bear the heart and soul of Christ, entering those dark places of the congregates/client's soul with the sword of the spirit, shrouded with the compassion and the love of Christ; I am to be *steel wrapped in velvet*.

TURNING THE PAGE: NEXT STEPS

Retirement came early for my husband and me. Major shifts in the economy placed some companies in positions to close or offer severance packages.

I was ready and looking forward to early retirement. I put in quite a few years working various shifts, holding various positions, all the while continuing my education. Even though I had put in many years at the pharmaceutical/bio-tech business, I somehow knew this was not it. Yes, it paid the bills, but there had to be more than this.

I loved my work. It was rewarding and gratifying to know the vaccines we formulated fought diseases of the body. For me, there was a yearning to do something else, something greater, something that did more than fight diseases of the body, but also the "dis-ease" that plagued the very soul of mankind.

This new chapter in my life fostered the need to further my education in psychotherapy; with a conviction and passion for the family, I pursued an education in marriage and family therapy.

I found this period in my life to be so fulfilling and rewarding. I committed myself to preaching and teaching the word of God not only in the church, but also ministering to those experiencing emotional and psychological pain through pastoral counseling and by performing the duties of a volunteer chaplain at the local sheriff's department. The biggest reward came by the way of not only the course work, but the mandatory 15 sessions of therapy as part of the curriculum.

Here I was, a volunteer chaplain ministering in the jail and a board-certified pastoral counselor, counseling individuals and families in need. I thought my education provided enough insight and processing; with all the journals and reflection paper assignments, to deal with my past trauma. I quickly became aware that was only the tip of the iceberg.

In therapy, I presented with a narrative saturated with shame, disappointment, and lack of agency, all stemming from an environment plagued with verbal and physical abuse. It's in therapy I came to realize that many of my past experiences continued to play out in my current life and my marriage. Therapy lasted two years beyond the 15-session requirement. I had a lot of work to do.

To continue to sharpen my clinical skills and to move closer to licensure, I took a position at a residential treatment center (RTC). During the interview, the hiring manager was intrigued with my overall work experience, and was particularly intrigued with how I, as a pastoral counselor, used the principles of marriage and family therapy in my pastoral counseling.

I was offered a position as a caseworker for a new program for adjudicated youth with problematic sexualized behaviors. After one year as a caseworker, I accepted the position of a family social worker. As a family social worker, I performed case work for juvenile offenders who committed sex offenses against minors (with a disposition of out-of-home placement).

Family therapy in this environment served to be a valuable part of treatment because it can be just as effective as individual therapy. Family therapy allowed me to observe their family dynamic in real time and provided me with a complete idea of what was happening within the life of the youth. It also provided a safe space for family members to process their thoughts and feelings around such a crisis. It was a very sad situation as some of these youths had been disowned by their families. The pain and the trauma were sometimes too much for the family to bear, as the families of these youth had all but abandoned them. For those families who tried to remain supportive, it was a difficult task and a lengthy process for reunification.

This was certainly challenging work; problematic sexualized behavior poses a complex challenge. Most of these youths were not only juvenile offenders, but also victims of circumstance who came from families who were functioning under high levels of stress, maltreatment, substance abuse, and domestic violence.

This is why family therapy is so important. If an individual is not well, the entire family is not well. I am a firm believer that an individual cannot be treated outside of the family. While holding such a position I had to be mindful of my own traumatic past, careful not to project my narrative on to the families.

I often wondered if the experiences in our lives sets the stage of God's sovereign plan. He prepares us and positions us for such a time as this. I would have never thought that I would be working with this population of youth. As I look back over my life, every situation, every circumstance, the good, the bad, and the indifferent was fashioning me for the purpose that God had for my life. As I reflect on the egregious acts that were inflicted upon me, a scripture comes to mind.

You meant evil against me, but God meant it for good (Genesis 50:20).

I often struggled with the latter half of this scripture, because how can any good come from such egregious acts? For it to take on the form of good, I had to take on a different perspective despite the tragic acts against me and see the bigger picture of God's divine plan for my life. It was my healing journey that changed my perspective and brought restoration through the act of forgiveness. This act of forgiveness served as a freeing agent of the emotional baggage that played out for many years in my life. God saw fit in placing me in positions where I could do the most good, where He would get the glory out of my life.

I was placed among individuals and families dealing with pain and despair. I certainly can relate to the scars of family dysfunction, but it is God's sovereign goodness that overrides all.

THE CYCLE OF ADDICTION

*I*t is said history repeats itself.

My husband and I are empty-nesters and have been for quite some time now. My oldest grandson is in his second year of college, I am semi-retired; and I operate a private practice that combines pastoral counseling and marriage and family therapy.

Two years into my practice disaster hit. The world was at war. Not a war with another country or nation, but a war of an invisible enemy. This enemy radically changed the lives of humankind.

Fear ruled the day—fear for oneself, family members, loss of employment, financial strain, and food insecurities. Stay-at-home orders fostered isolation from the outside world. Shut-down orders were in place for certain businesses and organizations and travel came to a screeching halt.

It was COVID-19, and it became the arch-nemesis of the world. Masks, face shields, and gloves became part of one's everyday wardrobe. Zoom became the chief vehicle of face-to-face communication. The embracing of a loved one, a friendly handshake, or a loving smile was far too scary and avoided.

An eerie silence now occupied the streets. Mornings consisted of getting up at 6:00 a.m. and standing in long lines outside grocery stores braving the cold to shop for groceries, but mostly for toilet paper, paper towels, and disinfectant as they were a hot commodity. It was a scary time, as there were shortages of food items and pharmaceuticals. Some items, such as chicken and cereals, were limited to two packs or boxes per family. I often wondered how a family of six could survive with these types of restrictions.

The COVID-19 pandemic forced the nation into a recession. Millions of people found themselves forced from their office to a life of remote work. The unemployment rate tripled surging to 13% as noted by the U.S. Bureau of Labor Statistics. Students were moved from the classroom to their living rooms as learning became remote and parents and caregivers became teacher assistants. The government was forced to aid the population in meeting the financial demands as the major stock indexes plummeted. Landlords were not getting rent, mortgages were not being paid, foreclosures flooded the courts, and the population was in dire straits. The world anxiously waited for help and healing, which would come by way of a vaccine.

The shutdown and stay-at-home orders only served as a breeding ground for depression, anxiety, and an increase in intimate partner violence and suicide. For those who struggled with mental health issues, isolation only served to further exacerbate their symptomatology.

One of my cases pushed me to a place that I thought I would never have to encounter. This client, who I will call Client Z, was unique, soft at heart, and definitely marched to the beat of a different drummer—some would say a little eccentric.

Client Z presented with grief and depression and had a history of troubled relationships and two failed marriages. Client Z didn't want "therapy."

"I just need someone to talk to, none of that therapy stuff," Client Z said.

This took some restraint on my part, as I found myself tempted to offer an alternative action to Client Z's reaction to certain situations. Whether Client Z realized it or not, we actually worked through some of the issues that Client Z experienced throughout life, especially around recent losses.

Client Z began to feel safe and confident enough to start socializing again, joined a church, got involved in a Bible study group, prayer group, and attended community events. Our conversations began to revolve around newfound faith and a renewed social life. Client Z often spoke about loneliness, and to address loneliness—with much convincing from a family member—Client Z adopted a puppy.

To manage depression, Client Z had a complete physical, and was prescribed a mild anti-depressant by their primary physician. Client Z attested that life was getting better, and our sessions were spent updating me on daily events and the gossip that circulated among the seniors at the senior center.

Then it happened. That invisible enemy, COVID-19, hit—and shut-down orders thrust us all into seclusion. For Client Z, that meant they were back from where they came, a place that was all too familiar: isolation.

As mental health facilities and programs closed their doors, individuals had nowhere to turn. Individuals turned to their local church, but most churches were forced to close their doors, as well. It appeared that even faith was of no use against this invisible enemy. Pastors and clergy were stretched to the max, as families turned to their pastors and clergy for comfort and solace.

Clients felt stranded and isolated, left to live out their problems in the streets, and going back to familiar coping mechanisms.

As a pastoral counselor and marriage and family therapist, I began to get more referrals. I took advantage of the use of technology to virtually meet the needs of clients, offering counseling and therapy via Zoom, Facetime, or WhatsApp. Some of my existing clients opted to wait it out rather than participating in sessions virtually.

We had new heroes during this period of time. Heroes took on a whole new look. The face of the hero had changed, and the frontlines where no longer restricted to the battle fields of the Armed Services. Frontline workers were those who showed up for their jobs in spite of the potential risk of their personal health to keep the rest of us safe.

This war took on a different appearance. Battle grounds were not in the fields but in the hospitals. Our frontline workers did not wear the typical army gear. These frontline workers wore scrubs, face shields, gloves, mask, and respirators. Our heroes took the form of nurses, doctors, healthcare professionals, and paramedics. They were on the frontlines fighting a war with an invisible enemy, who did not discriminate. The entire world was at war.

Clergy took a position on the frontlines, as well. With the shutdown of churches, clergy made themselves available, receiving calls for prayer and visiting hospitals despite heavy restrictions. They prayed for dying loved ones and their families. Pastors and clergy were checking in and shopping for the elderly, protecting this vulnerable population.

I continued to receive referrals and calls from individuals looking for a therapist. As one individual shared, their therapist told them, "See you after COVID," obviously not realizing that we were in it for the long haul and at this point in time there was no end in sight.

My calendar filled up quickly, especially with parents calling on behalf of their children, as children were impacted as much by this pandemic as adults. Children and young adults presented with anxiety, sadness, and fear. This was a very scary time for not only the United States of America, but also for the entire world.

The news channels were bombarded with COVID-19 deaths, and the numbers were astronomical. Every day the death toll continued to rise. It spread like wildfire and there was no stopping it. My heart was moved with compassion for all those who had lost loved ones to COVID-19. No one escaped the impact of COVID-19, whether it was their friends, peers, co-workers, family members, and even clients—this pandemic did not discriminate.

One Friday, it was time for my afternoon session with Client Z. I called and got no answer. I was a little concerned as the previous Sunday Client Z called upset and in distress. They were not faring well with all that was happening in the world, and the isolation was getting too hard to bear. The shut in-orders served to exasperate their symptoms of depression and anxiety. Client Z sounded somewhat disoriented, and speech was pressured.

I attempted to assess what was happening, and Client Z let me know that they had been drinking alcohol, which they would do on occasion. I immediately attempted to assess just how much alcohol was ingested and was any medication taken. I instructed Client Z to call their daughter, as their daughter lived on the next street, and would check in with Client Z on a daily basis. They explained that they had reached out to their daughter, and their daughter got annoyed with them, as the conversation did not go well. Client Z stated that they were going to be okay. The conversation ended with Client Z stating that they would play some Christian music and go to bed.

I made a second attempt to reach Client Z, with no success. It was not like them to miss an appointment. I thought about them all weekend. Unfortunately, I did not have any other number to call.

On Monday morning, I received a phone call from Client Z's daughter. When I answered the phone, they immediately identified themselves and offered an apology.

My heart sunk.

Client Z's daughter shared that they too had not heard from Client Z. When they got no response, they came that morning to check in. They found Client Z, on the floor. Client Z had passed away.

I was shocked and couldn't speak for a moment. I extended my sincere apologies and said if they needed anything to please contact me. The daughter said thank you and hung up.

I stood silent for a moment as tears began to stream down my face. My husband came into the room.

"Are you OK?" he asked.

"No, I just lost a client," I said.

"What do you mean?" he asked.

"I assume an overdose," I said, then burst into tears.

My husband gave me a hug, and I told him I needed a moment. I went to my office and cried. There were two plants in my office that Client Z had given me, one for my birthday and another for

Christmas. As I looked at them, I thought on our sessions and what Client Z brought to this therapeutic relationship.

This was hard, Lord, this was really hard.

I took the week off. I needed space to process and to work through the flood of emotions that I was experiencing. It was a week of crying, praying, blaming (myself), and questioning my clinical skills. I looked over the case file every day.

What did I miss, what could I have said that Sunday? We were on the phone for over an hour, what could I have said that would have helped them feel better?

I began to think maybe Client Z's longing to be with Jesus was more than in jest. We all long to see our Savior one day in glory. Maybe Z's longing was more than idle words, but a strong literal desire to be with Jesus. Why didn't I catch that?

I beat myself up for weeks, I even prayed asking God, why didn't He show me or tell me. Maybe He did, and I didn't hear Him. I prayed for God's mercy and healing of my heart. I thank God for my family prayer line. We meet bi-weekly for prayer and Bible study. This was a time that I needed the prayers and support of family. I didn't have to go through this alone. Thank God for my family.

There is never a good time for this kind of situation. This just added more weight to my ongoing sorrow—sorrow regarding my prodigal son. There was a deep sadness and a concern close to my heart: my son. My son was out in the world, a world filled with COVID-19, homeless and destitute.

It was a little over two years, with very little contact with the family, since my son had distanced himself from us all. Every now and then we would hear from him, whether for money or food. What hurt the most was that my son had dropped out of his son's life. He had become destitute—living on the streets, one might say. His condo was no longer the home that it was designed to be. It had become a den of addiction and death, leading to eviction and foreclosure. This is not the dream that I had for my son, or for any of my sons.

I would hear things about my son from various people who saw him in passing. It did not serve my heart well. This was my son, my child. No matter how old they are, they are always your child. A mother's heart aches when her children are in emotional pain. I often wonder what happened to the close bond that we once shared. It seemed like yesterday we were working at the same pharmaceutical facility, and we would have conversation about life and about God. Things happened so fast. It was like I woke up one morning and things had drastically changed.

My son, my beloved son, had distanced himself from the life from which he was raised. It was painful to have my grandson call and ask if I had heard from his dad. My grandson became angry, very angry. What lay beneath that anger was a deep sadness and rejection.

I remember one day picking up my grandson to take him to the store. My other sons and I would make concerted efforts to reach out and spend time with him. His uncles took on the "father role" in their brother's absence, but for him it never filled that void that only his father could fill. As we drove to the store, I thought it would be a good time to let him know that his father was in a bad place in his life. I explained to him what addiction does to an individual and to one's family. I apologized but made no excuses for his father's absence.

All the while I was speaking, my grandson continued to look out of the passenger window. There was a moment of silence. Then he spoke.

"All this time I thought it was me, I thought he didn't want me anymore," he said.

At this point my grandson was a teenager, not a little kid. He had carried this script for years. It brought tears to my eyes, and once again I became angry with my son. Why is it that people don't understand that it is the child that always suffers in situations like this? When a parent becomes absent, it's not just about them, it is the child that internalizes disappointment and rejection.

With the onset of the pandemic, most hotels that provided lodging for individuals receiving housing assistance requested relocation of these tenants, pretty much evicting them and leaving them virtually homeless. Where could they possibly go? With everyone sheltering in place, the real estate market coming to a standstill. My son was among those impacted by this order.

There were many nights that sleep did not come easy for me. As I lay awake looking at the ceiling, my mind raced with painful thoughts.

Where is my son, is he okay? I know that he is a grown man and chose this life. Sometimes I wonder if this life chose him. Did my son fall victim to the generational curse of addiction that ran through the family tree?

I'm sure that people mean well when they attempt to offer encouragement, such as *"Weeping may endure for a night, but joy cometh in the morning"* (Psalm 30:5, KJV). It seemed morning would never come. *Oh, woman of God where is your faith? I know who I am, a pastoral counselor, a marriage and family therapist—but I am also a mother, a mother that continues to grieve the loss of her son. I speak of a severed mother and son relationship, the most painful kind.*

Thoughts often raced through my head. Where did I go wrong? I rehearsed the promises of God, such as, *"Believe on the Lord Jesus Christ, and you will be saved, you and your household"* (Acts 16:31-34). I prayed, fasted, and cried for the soul of my child, yet my prayers went unanswered. My sons were at every shut-in, right by my side at prayers services, and they were placed on the altar in daily prayers. *Where are my tears, a mother's tears of anguish? Did you not say that you save every tear in a bottle? Why are you saving them? What is the response to the many tears?*

At night, I lay in a fetal position, crumpled on the floor, worried sick, crying out to the Lord to take this pain away. I could no longer relax to the sound of rain hitting against my windowpanes—it no longer served as calm or "good sleeping weather." The sound of light rain that filled the atmosphere no longer brought peace, it only brought pain as I wondered if my son was sheltered from the storm.

I prayed in the winter months, praying for a mild winter. Stories of abandoned buildings serving as shelter, nights of sleeping in bus terminals; I dug deep within my soul to find words to express my pain but all I could muster up were groans. I cried unto the Lord, "Please, I want my son safe. I come heavy laden, but you, Lord, promised rest."

My response to the people's stories about my son were thoughts like *I don't want to hear any more stories, why are you telling me these stories, do you understand the pain that these stories bring. I closed my ears for the sake of my heart. Lord, please. This is a cup I can no longer bear.*

What is it about addiction that goes beyond the physical and mental dimension to the breaking of one's spirit, the very essence of who God created one to be? It definitely comes between the God and man relationship. I have come to the knowledge that addiction is not just a disease of the individual but a disease of the family, as well. Addiction affects the body, mind, spirit, and social relations. It takes on the persona of hopelessness and helplessness. It's not about chasing the next high, it's chasing the next thing that will alleviate the emotional pain and cope with the stressors of life.

When I look back on my husband's past addiction (clean for over 30 years) and my son's addiction, (clean for four years) was I so blind not to see the emotional pain and stressors in their lives? Thinking on both of their lives, I saw there were signs of low self-esteem, placatory and non-confrontational. It wasn't until his late thirties that my son disclosed that he suffered from bouts of depression. He described it like feeling dead inside, just lying staring into space.

It hurt to hear stories of his emotional struggles. I didn't get it. He was making good money working in the pharmaceutical industry, driving an expensive car, and living in a condo, but all the while, he was broken inside. He shared that everyone thought he was doing great, but deep inside he was struggling with a deep sadness, an emptiness for which he could not find the words. Who knows what lies deep in one's subconscious; no one can see the invisible wounds that a person has endured.

Again, I questioned my prayer life and faith. I prayed, read, fasted and still my family was under attack, I'm still asking myself why my prayers are going unanswered. I dared not judge God, nor did I get angry with Him. I remember my grandmother saying you never question God.

"Ours is not to wonder why, ours is just to do and die," she'd say.

That never sat well with me, as there are individuals in the Bible that got angry with God. Jonah, David, Job—all individuals of faith—and one referenced as the apple of God's eye. What I can do is be angry and sin not. What I tasked myself to do is trust God and know that He will answer my prayers in His own way and own time. I had to take stock in the fact that individuals have a free will and things happen based on the choices that we make in life. I'm not in control of another person's destiny. Who knows the will of God but God Himself? I must position myself in constant prayer to prepare myself for God's perfect timing.

I always encouraged my sons to surround themselves with positive people, those that will pull them up, not pull them down. Because my eldest always struggled with self-esteem issues, he worked hard at presenting himself as very self-confident. It was ironic that he would gravitate to individuals—I say this carefully—not on his level, those who were unemployed, drug users, those who were of the streets. I guess it made him feel good about himself.

These associates, or as he referred to them, friends, took advantage of his naivete. My son was raised in the church and taught to love and to serve those who are less fortunate. Unfortunately, my son tried to "save" these so-called friends within his own strength, rather than the strength of God. They affirmed him, gave him accolades of how successful and smart he was, all the time fleecing his pockets. When he himself fell victim to their abuse, they abandoned him.

When he became destitute, where were they? Where was the reciprocity? He did all the giving, getting nothing in return but a false sense of self-worth. This had a profound effect on my son's emotional and psychological well-being. The deep-seated hurt and betrayal led to a hardened heart and serious trust issues. These experiences only served to exacerbate his low-self-worth, attributing to his use of drugs;

all this leading to traumatic experiences, depression, and post-traumatic stress disorder.

My son was in crisis, my family was in crisis once again. He was not only a son, but he was also a brother, father, nephew, and a cousin. This was a family affair. I needed to navigate through this much differently than in the past, as I had done with my husband, where I sat in judgment, exercising a self-righteous behavior. This was self-destructive behavior against one's very soul, and against the heart of the family.

As God's creation, we are comprised of mind, body, soul, and spirit. To serve my son well, I must learn to minister to his mind, body, soul, and spirit. My son needed not only my prayers, but my compassion and empathy by way of God's Word. I needed to get an understanding of the mental and psychological pieces that were playing out in his life.

I concluded that prayer and trusting in God was key in helping my son's journey to healing. I needed to learn more, to understand more. I needed an understanding of his entire being, for it is the healing of the whole man that brings true deliverance. As for me, this was a season of continued growth and development as well as sustainability. I cried a lot of tears through the years, and my heart has endured a lot of pain, but it was my continued trust in God that renewed my strength and relieved me of the guilt of failure regarding my son.

In hindsight it was my son's addiction and traumatic experiences that played a huge role in my decision for furthering my education relative to psychotherapy.

The stabilization of family is important as families are the very core of our communities, playing a crucial role in social development. Families are responsible for the development of their children, instilling ethical values of citizenship and belonging to society. As a survivor of physical and sexual abuse stemming from family dysfunction, I have a passion and conviction for the healing of not just the individual, but the family, as well.

But with this conviction came the realization that there was a need for me to heal from the dysfunction of my own family of origin.

A Narrative
Re-Examined

"Restore to me the joy of Your salvation,
And uphold me by Your generous Spirit"
(Psalm 51:12, NKJV).

My journey leading up to certification in pastoral counseling and licensing in marriage and family therapy was preceded by years of emotional and physical abuse. Being an adult child of an alcoholic (ACOA) left me with unresolved feelings of sadness, fear, and anxiety which played out well into my adulthood. There was a lot of mending and healing needed. How could I minister or counsel anyone with so much of my own emotional baggage? In order to enter the dark places with my clients, I needed to work through the dark places that I had stuffed away for years. As a Pastoral Counselor and Marriage and Family therapist, I cannot expect to take anyone where I have not gone myself or where I am not willing to go. I had to work through the pain and change the negative scripts that I had come to live by.

I had let my past define who I was, which was contrary to who God had created and called me to be. It was not easy to peel away the many labels that I had affixed to my person. These negative scripts were so ingrained that I could not see myself as anything else. It was unfortunate that my family of origin lacked the positive affirmation that is effective in nurturing emotional well-being. If only there were acts of kindness and love, I would have the self-esteem and self-belief that would carry one throughout life.

Despite it all, it was God's will that prevailed. They said I would never speak, but now I speak before audiences. I was hidden in the closet of darkness, not allowed to see the light of the day, but I am set free from darkness and now witness Jesus as the light of the world. They deemed me weak and fragile, but now I stand strong in the face of adversity. This could only be possible through the love of God and taking charge of my mental wellness, fulfilling the purpose that God had for my life.

It was now time for a re-examination of the early chapters of my life. I was not looking to rewrite the early chapters. Can anyone rewrite her own history or "herstory?" What I desired to do is search for the true meaning and purpose of my life, a "repurposing," if I can call it that.

Rather than it being a narrative solely of fear, brokenness, and despair, it could be a narrative of resilience, survival, and safety, filled with words of a renewed sense of self, faith, strength, and endurance. For it was up to me to exercise my ability to choose how to respond to all the painful experiences in my life. Whether I chose to respond with fear, bitterness, and unforgiveness—or respond with a forgiving heart and with purpose.

This repurposing, as I call it, would require a transformation of the mind, challenging those ingrained negative scripts. It would require viewing my past through a different lens and tending to the matters of the heart.

There is undoubtedly fear of casting a light on one's past. Who knows what is hidden in the dark corners of one's heart?

Sexual, physical, and emotional abuse were the experiences that served to be most traumatic for me. These experiences became deeply etched in my mind and deep in my heart, distorting my sense of self. It only served to shape my view about God, myself, and the world.

My view of God was reflective of my relationship with my father: distant and invisible. For me the world was unjust and unfair, and I found myself merely existing not living. I felt that I was wandering aimlessly through life, scared and useless.

It's not that I crawled in a corner, but I did do what most people do: I worked and began burying myself into education and studying. I had this need to search—for what I didn't know. Whatever it was, I needed it. The longing was like no other. I likened it to longing for a cold drink in the heat of summer. Nothing else will satisfy that longing or quench that thirst. You long for it, you envision it, you can almost taste it. Once you get that cold drink in your hands, the anticipation is almost too hard to bear. Every part of your body is reacting, aching with anticipation as it touches your lips, then your tongue, and slides down your throat. The coolness ripples through every part of your body and you let out a sigh of relief, signaling satisfaction and relief.

But this longing was not a physical longing, it was deeper than that. A cold drink fell very short of quenching this inner thirst of my soul. This was a thirst for meaning and purpose that no cold drink could satisfy.

How does anyone make sense of sexual abuse? What meaning and purpose can come from any type of abuse, for that matter. It was so hard seeing another side of this, but I could no longer live in a state of hate and victim hood.

It takes a lot of emotional energy to maintain this burden. I certainly do not have a patent on sexual trauma, and I am sure that I am not alone in asking the big question "Why?" Why does it appear that God looked another way? If God is all knowing, all seeing, did He not witness these acts?

What comes to mind is the biblical narrative of Hagar, Sarah's handmaid (Genesis 16). Hagar suffered abuse at the hand of Sarah her mistress, so much so that Hagar was forced to flee.

Hagar finds herself in the wilderness near a well. God acknowledges her despair and hears the cries of her son. What God instructs next is so powerful. God instructs her to return and submit herself because this was not the end of her narrative. Great things were in store for Hagar and her offspring. The angel of God met Hagar where she was, He saw her pain and despair. *"You are God who sees; for she said, Have I not even here* (in the wilderness) *remained alive after seeing Him* (who sees me with understanding and compassion)" (Genesis 16:13 AMP Bible.)

How could I ever think that such a loving and compassionate God could turn His back on my pain? How could I hold these egregious acts against a gracious, loving God, who sacrificed His own son that I may have life, a life that is not void of evil, but a life that is eternal?

God created a world that was good. The Bible tells us in the beginning God looked upon His creation and noted that it was *"very good"* (Genesis 1:31). It's a known fact that evil is present in the world, and there are people who do evil things. God saw my pain and held my tears near to His heart.

Therefore, it took an earnest effort on my part in seeking God's comfort and a commitment to participating in therapy. The combination of both disciplines, pastoral counseling and psychotherapy, helped me to reconcile the good and evil that is ever present in this world—but more importantly the evil that had occurred in my life. I wondered if it had been a little easier to reconcile if these acts were perpetrated by a stranger? This is not to minimize or discount sexual abuse against any victim. Any form of abuse is traumatic, but when it's committed by a family member, that goes against every moral standard of what constitutes a family.

How do I repurpose a narrative of such a repulsive and evil act? Is reframing even possible? I needed to put my life under a microscope, I needed to re-examine every part, every aspect. There had to be a deeper meaning. This is not the truth; this could not be it—a life filled with pain and fear could not be my destiny.

I wrote, I journaled, I had to get it out of my head and onto paper in order to get a better perspective, to see it outside of myself. There needed to be a "repurposing" of my problem-saturated story, a story dripping with pain and shame. My original narrative was intended to keep me stuck in victimhood, stuck in depression, fear, and anxiety. The pain was great, and I could no longer endure the turmoil within my spirit. I needed to be free. I needed to go from surviving to thriving.

There seemed to be a tug of war within my spirit. Why was it so hard to let go of the pain? Pain had its grip on my very being. I reciprocated with intensity. It was difficult not to "hold onto" the pain. Strongholds had their grip on me, but I, too, had my grip on the pain.

Holding on to the pain seemed to serve a purpose for me. With the pain came defensive structures that I built to protect me. I possessed the will to control every situation and trust no one as it would only lead to hurt and pain. Here I was thinking that I was in control. Little did I know I had no control at all.

With a "repurposing" my narrative would take on a new purpose. My testimony would become the vehicle of overcoming defensiveness and barriers. My healing journey helped to weaken my grip on the pain that prevented me in becoming my true self, the me that I was created and called to be.

It is the telling of my story that continues to bring healing as it fosters a narrative of hope and restoration. Telling my story helped me to work through my sexual and emotional trauma. It helped me in getting a clearer picture of my past and how it played out in my life. It helped me to gain an understanding that it spoke more about those who hurt me than it did about me.

My narrative has gone from a story of despair to a narrative filled with hope. In reconstructing my storyline, it provided the opportunity to find meaning in my experiences.

Using narrative therapy, as a spiritual practice, helped me to detach from the dominant story of my life, trauma. Detaching from this negative narrative, allowed a new narrative to spring forth, which is a life-giving transformation.

I began to separate myself from the problem, removing those trauma-applied labels, challenging those negative scripts and unhealthy beliefs. With the Lord's help, I became empowered to make changes in my thought process and my behavioral patterns.

Did it happen overnight? Of course not. It took persistence and some serious humbling of the spirit.

What I appreciated by this approach was that it allowed me to continue to "write" my story, a story with a future that reflects who God created me to be, and the me I desired to be. My capabilities and the true purpose for my life shines through the words of my story. It's a narrative that helped me to see that what happened to me does not define me. It is a narrative that helped me to process and see just how my traumatic experiences were playing out in my life.

I soon recognized that these circumstances not only affected my mind but my heart as well, hardening my heart with anger and resentment.

I would like to note that the mind and heart are intimately connected and are often referenced as the seat of life or strength. The heart is said to be the seat to all emotions. Maybe that is why the heart is so important to God. It's a clean heart that is important in having a true relationship with God. When we turn to God, it is He who cleanses our heart and gives us a new heart.

I can honestly say that as much as I attested that I gave God my heart, I struggled with an unforgiving heart for some time. What boggles my mind is what God saw in my heart didn't change the love that He has for me. God judges the intents of the heart, and if our intentions are not pure, He loves us so much that He corrects us. To be receptive to correction, one must be humble enough to recognize the error of their ways and heed the correction.

It was humility that allowed me to become teachable. It paved the way for me to receive God's direction, correction, and His grace. When we receive God's grace and His forgiveness, as grace and forgiveness operate together, it requires us to extend God's grace and forgiveness to others.

Forgiveness was the biggest and the hardest hurdle in my healing journey. Breeding unforgiveness kept me stuck in my childhood, keeping alive that wounded little girl who grew up to be an angry young woman. I remained locked in negativity, refusing to grow up emotionally and psychologically. I never realized that when we hold grudges and unforgiveness, that we only hold on to the negative part of the individual, we never see the positive part.

When I think about my relationship with my mother, I realized that I was holding onto a fantasy for many years of hope, hope for a mother-daughter relationship. That relational dynamic did not come until well in my adulthood. I had come to realize that I was no longer that little girl who was dependent on a mother's love. I had already resolved that I was never "Daddy's little girl," but it took some time to realize that this mother-daughter relationship wasn't one that I would ever have.

I was now an adult who had the power and the responsibility to fashion my life. It was only when I moved from victimhood and empathized with my mother's story that I made space for forgiveness. This is why I believe I was ready to confront the other issues in my life.

Parent wounds run deep. If I could release this pain, it would make space in my heart to forgive those who inflicted hurt and pain upon me. Some say confront your abuser, but for me, why run the risk of having more pain afflicted upon me? If I confront, what if they don't receive or validate my feelings? I have no control over how they will respond, but I do have control over how I respond to their response. It was time for me to face these demons of the past and confront my fears.

Another component in my healing journey was therapy. It proved beneficial as it helped me release the repressed emotions of my trauma. It provided a safe space, which gave me a voice to express my hurts and pains. Therapy also taught me how to sit with my emotions, validate them, and process through them. I also learned how to recognize triggers and the emotions that came with them. I asked myself, where have I felt this way before—assessing if those emotions belonged in the present or in the past. There needed to be a release along with this process. Journaling works well for me, but also letter writing was a form of releasing all those emotions and gave me a voice.

To: *The Author of My Pain*

As I write this letter to you, my heart is pounding, feels like it is coming out of my chest. My stomach is in knots, it's like I have come face to face with you (ground and breath). As I am writing I am flooded with emotions. After all these years, my body still reacts with anxiety and tension. You are not even here but tell that to my stomach.

It really stinks that home was not a safe place. You certainly didn't make it any better. That is why I was hell-bent on ensuring my home was a safe place for my family, but it came with a price. My family paid the price of the ill that was done to me. They were forced to live in a controlling, domineering environment, controlled by my quest to have the perfect family. My low self-worth and a lack of a sense of self was the star of the show. The burden of abuse weighed heavily upon me. Anger became my bedfellow, fear and mistrust played a major role in my life.

What did you think would happen to me psychologically and emotionally. You ruined me, you destroyed my sense of self. You took no thought about how your actions would affect me. Thank you for years of gastrointestinal problems, and don't forget all the dysfunctional relationships as a result of the abuse.

Did you not know that sexual abuse serves to teach that anything goes when it comes to sex, with no repercussions? I allowed myself to be manipulated in acts that are too embarrassing to speak of. I owe all this to you, thank you.

Am I being a little sarcastic? Yes. I am flooded with emotions. I ask myself time and time again, why am I in such a state as this? I have to reflect, although it hurts, and heal.

It is like a double-edged sword, it's either deal and heal, or live life in fear and despair. You stripped me of any sense of self. I felt worthless, dirty, shamed. Yes, I was broken, but thank God as the Bible says, He saved all my tears, and they did not go to waste. It was through God's grace that my life was placed on the path to healing. I am no longer a victim, but I am victorious, for everything you meant for evil, God turned it for my good.

I am not casting this letter in the sea of forgetfulness, but into the sea of forgiveness. By forgiving you, it releases the chains of bondage from my soul. It's those chains that had me bound in the dark corners of my soul.

Let me tell you of a dream that I had.

I saw darkness all around me, I felt my heart pounding as fear began to grip me. I could not speak, I just stared into the darkness. Then something happened, my heart was not beating as fast, there seemed to be a calm slowly taking over. Then, just like a window shade slowly lifts to let the light of day in, darkness began to shrink as light slowly took over. As I looked toward the darkness, light slowly began to appear, it was as bright as the sun. I kept my eyes toward the light, losing sight of the darkness that once occupied the space. There is light in the midst of darkness.

As I moved from those dark corners of my soul, I felt and bear witness of the love of God. As I look back on the days that I had fallen, I know it was God that picked me up. Looking back, it was

God's hands that I see during this journey. When things were clouded with little understanding it was the lamp and light of God that paved the way.

I am forever grateful for the grace and love that God has bestowed upon me. I continue to take a backward look at the cross, reminiscent of the work that was accomplished. I take a forward look for what is to come: hope and restoration.

IT HAPPENED AT CALVARY

Pastoral counseling is a counseling that aims at the heart of the matter. It deals with the spiritual, emotional, and psychological aspects of an individual. When I speak of psychotherapy, specifically marriage and family therapy, it is a therapy that aims at the core of the family dynamic to foster a more intimate and nurturing environment. If we take a closer look, they definitely have more in common than differences.

I always wanted to teach in some capacity, as education is very important to me. I loved learning and acquiring knowledge, and I've never gotten above learning. I excelled in school and college, not sure if it was proving a point or self-validation. Whatever it was, I pushed for higher learning. I always felt no one should ever get above learning. Learning aides us in growth, improvement, and evolving as individuals. Knowledge sharpens our skills relative to reasoning and problem-solving.

A strong knowledge base has proven to help the brain function more effectively. Life knowledge is important and useful in day-to-day events. The Bible notes, *"Wisdom brings strength, and knowledge gives power. Battles are won by listening to advice and making a lot of plans. Wisdom is too much for fools"* (Proverbs 24: 5-6, Contemporary English Version). I often thought, *what is the sense for acquiring knowledge if we are not willing to share it?* They say knowledge is power, but others say the power lies in the sharing of knowledge.

I never imagined that my passion for teaching would come by the way of ministry and psychotherapy/psychoeducation. I desired to do more than speak about the benefits of an integrative approach that today's pastoral counseling provides. I want others to share in the benefits and the uniqueness that today's pastoral counseling brings to any counseling/therapeutic process. I know this is the path that God placed me on. A path that helps me to gain a better understanding of myself and making sense of my family trauma, along with a conviction in using this knowledge and insight to help others. It is not in any way to replace one's biblical counseling services, but to glean from today's pastoral counseling. Incorporating the principals of psychotherapy provides a more robust counseling experience. As we are still dealing with a mental health crisis post-COVID-19, especially among our teens and young adults, my appeal is to the church to look at such an approach with an open heart.

The integration of pastoral counseling with psychotherapy has served to provide an effective approach to my therapeutic process, without the loss of the theological foundation of pastoral counseling.

As a Pastoral Counselor and MFT, I understand that we are not only physical beings but emotional and spiritual beings, as well. As a pastoral counselor I deal with the spirit of man, the part of that inner life in relation to God. But humans are also mental beings as well, and this is where psychotherapy can come into play. With a careful balance between biblical counseling and today's pastoral counseling, the inclusion of psychotherapy can offer clients and congregates, as well as yourself, a holistic approach to their counseling experience.

I have been in church for many years. I was 26 years of age when I gave my heart to the Lord. I have witnessed and have been exposed to various doctrines, from prohibiting the wearing of pants and jewelry, to restriction of the movies and amusement parks—and have been told, "don't even think about going to a pool in the hot summer." Women only occupied leadership positions if they were under the leadership of a man. As far as any mental health issues it was attributed to some sort of evil or demonic spirit and any struggle was coined as a lack of faith. I have witnessed many deliverance services. Those individuals seeking deliverance would surrender their issues to God.

But I noticed at times that some of those individuals that were "delivered" were still struggling with the issue that they claimed deliverance from. How did I draw this conclusion? Some became my clients, not just from my place of worship, but from other churches as well. These clients presented with the very issues they were seeking deliverance from.

I am certainly not dismissing prayer or one's deliverance services, but what happens when one is "delivered" from alcohol, drug addiction, pornography, or depression. What does the individual do with the impulsivity related to addiction and pornography or the trauma that is related to the depression?

For me, relative to my "deliverance," I believe that God opened the door of my soul to foster healing and to be filled with more of Him. When deliverance came, the door of my soul was opened. I felt exposed and vulnerable, and all my brokenness lay in front of me. While there were mixed emotions, it was a feeling of release. I was left with all the emotions associated with my trauma flooding to the forefront. God opened the flood gates for true healing to take place.

God knew what I stood in need of, and I was now aware of what I needed to hand over to God and the situations that warranted forgiveness. Unforgiveness hardened my heart and had me chained to the past. I was deeply wounded and walls of defenses were thick—I could not, and I chose not to show love. With walls so thick nothing can go out and nothing can come in, either. I needed to draw closer to God and His love. God's love could break every wall and every chain that had me bound to the past.

God provided another component to this healing journey, and that was therapy. God afforded me this opportunity to work through the traumas I had endured through the early years of my life. I was able to gain an understanding, that I was not broken—I had deep-seated anger, and that I was not crazy—I had earned it rightly. My views, perspectives, and emotions were all tangled up in my family of origin dysfunction, which did not start with me but generations ahead of me.

God desires to heal us of our past traumas and all the emotions associated with it. When we experience mental health issues, deliverance aides in revealing the greater issue behind these symptoms. This is where psychotherapy can aide in getting to the root of the presenting issue.

I likened my deep-seated anger to the iceberg that struck the Titanic. The drivers of the ship only saw the tip of the iceberg and based their assessment on what they saw at the surface. They failed to take into consideration what they didn't see, what lay under the surface. My anger was only the tip of the iceberg; what lay beneath the anger were symptoms of anxiety, sadness, fear, and betrayal.

Another analogy I use comes from my family of origin. Growing up, I had a large backyard. In the summer months to aide in yard maintenance, we were tasked with pulling up the dandelions. We spent hours in the yard pulling up dandelions, only plucking the tops off. In a day or two, it was like we had done nothing at all, and the yard was full of dandelions again. We never realized—neither did my parents—that dandelions have roots that are up to 3 feet deep.

That's how I likened trauma. We can deal with what is in view, but we need to get to the root of the problem, the deep-seated trauma, which breeds various mood disorders. The root of my presenting issues were years of emotional and physical abuse. It was a family dynamic that bred dysfunction, and like my family of origin, these are the families I wish to serve.

As a pastoral counselor and marriage and family therapist, I have a passion and conviction to share the knowledge that I gleaned from today's pastoral counseling with my current religious institution and other religious institutions as well. I have exercised an integrated approach within my private practice for several years, taking a bio-psycho-social-spiritual approach and it has served my clients well.

Much to my surprise, when having conversations with some of my peers regarding mental health and the church, there was some skepticism. There were questions of utilizing any type of psychology or psychotherapy in the church, like there was no room for it. Even in discussing the possibility of integrating one's biblical counseling with today's pastoral counseling with some of my peers, there appeared to be some hesitation. This hesitation may have been due to inaccurate or a nonexistent understanding of the current capabilities of today's pastoral counseling. It's this hesitation and skepticism that prompted me to focus my doctoral thesis on this topic.

If we take a careful look at scripture and psychology, both are complimentary to each other. We have come to understand that one's spirituality is a source of strength. Psychology provides insight into our emotional and mental dynamic of our experience. The Bible instructs how we can become more emotionally and spiritually healthy. God has given us all things that pertain to life. Psychology casts light upon understanding human emotional experiences, helping individuals to cope with life and relationships. Combined, they both provide a source of inspiration and strength, which promotes change in the individual and the family.

Whether a Pastoral Counselor or Marriage and Family Therapist, both have committed to do no harm with a heart for the well-being of their congregate/client. Bringing comfort and restoration to the heart, mind, body and soul.

MAMA CC; DEATH BY CHOCOLATE

It is said that ministry starts at home, so why not start at my home church? As part of my research, I conducted interviews and focus groups within my local church, which I will call BCB, to get some thoughts and feedback for such in integrative approach. I was curious as to what type of counseling was being provided for the congregates. When I became a member of the church, I introduced myself to one of the senior members of the church. She introduced herself as Mama

CC. She had such a sweet disposition, and as a long-standing member she possessed a wealth of knowledge.

Mama CC was very active in the church. She held several senior positions within church auxiliaries. Mama CC was happy to share the history of the church she had called home for over a decade. She shared that it was the preaching that was instrumental in shaping one's spiritual growth and development. It was also Sunday School and Bible Studies that served to provide theological education. It was the women's and men's ministries that encouraged and fostered engagement in activities for the building of the kingdom of God. Mama CC said that these ministries provided a sense of connectedness and community among the congregates. As I listened to Mama CC, I sensed that congregates of BCB were secure in their relationship with Christ and committed to the work of ministry. BCB took pride in their community outreach programs, servicing not only the community but congregate needs as well.

It was a routine practice to respond to community crisis, as BCB played an active role in the distribution of supplies during the COVID-19 pandemic. As one of the new members of BCB, I have witnessed the cohesiveness of this congregation. After benediction I would spend time observing the congregates and engaging in fellowship as well. No one seemed to hurry out the door. Most would greet each other, sit, and have conversations, as children would be running around the church laughing and playing. One thing that stood out to me was families. Most were somehow related, whether biologically or through marriage.

As I reflect on the various churches where I fellowshipped, they were all very family-oriented; each congregation was made up of multiple families. It is these families which make up what we call a "church family." Just as families go through life together, so do the believers of Christ. The body of believers experience the ups and downs as any other family. Just as the family lends its support to one another, so does the family of believers, sharing in the joys and the sorrows of their fellow congregates.

This is how Mama CC presented BCB, a body of believers that not only attended church together but shared in the fullness of faith and life together and united by Christ as a family.

I have witnessed that strong sense of community over the various fellowship services and the meals that followed some of those services. It was plain to see that food is a huge part of the life of the church. What church do you know that true fellowship never happened over a good plate of food? No matter what you were going through, what issue you had as you entered the church, words of encouragement were sealed with a good plate of home cooking after service, and your problems seemed to melt away.

Oh, I can't forget about the desserts. Mama CC was well known for her desserts, including Sweet Potato Jacks, 7up Cake, and more notably, "Death by Chocolate." I love chocolate. If death comes by chocolate, this is the way you want to go.

Meals with my fellow brothers and sisters in Christ provided a deeper fellowship, not just meeting the spiritual needs but the emotional needs as well. Fellowship over a meal provides an opportunity to share in the goodness of the Lord, conversations that enrich the soul and enlighten the spirit. Being part of a church community can be a source of emotional and psychological support to those experiencing pain and hardship.

During Mama CC's tenure at BCB, she witnessed quite a few changes within the walls of the church, more specifically among leadership. There was one major crisis that put a wedge between the congregation—the re-building of one of the walls of the church. The wall was no longer structurally sound and posed a serious safety issue. The entire congregation was forced to find another place of worship. This also caused a huge financial burden for the church. It was a year and a half that the congregation lost their place of worship and what some called "home."

It was unfortunate that during this time some congregates chose alternate places of worship and did not return. This did not stop the huge re-opening celebration. With the wall complete a huge celebration was in order as their beloved BCB was restored. There was a march around the block back to the steps of BCB, a proud and joyous moment.

This joyous occasion was overshadowed by the number of changes in pastoral leadership, the hardest being the abandonment of their senior pastor. Each of these situations, from the loss of members, displacement, and unexpected retirement of their senior pastor, resulted in disappointment and sadness.

Change never comes easy but change is necessary for continued growth and development. But for BCB, these changes brought division and conflict. As Mama CC shared her narrative, you could hear the emotion in her voice. Relationships had been severed, and the "family" had been divided. BCB had lost its sense of safety and security.

After spending 10 to 20 years as a congregate, or as some say, being raised in the church, it is hard to institute change. Even positive change can be upsetting.

I wanted to get Mama CC's take and understanding of the impact that these changes had on the congregates emotional and spiritual state. Mama CC spoke of how each crisis brought various emotions among the congregates. Shifts in leadership caused congregates to grow weary of constant change, and the shifts in leadership caused an environment of instability. There was a time when tensions mounted so much so that it resulted in division among the congregates. This tension eventually led to the church splitting.

This definitely had a profound effect on the congregates emotional and psychological well-being. As Mama CC spoke about the tension and division, she missed that sense of community and togetherness that once was. I asked Mama CC what she and the other congregates did with the emotions that are tied to grief and abandonment. Mama CC shared that at times like this you turned to family, relying on them for support and comfort.

"But what about leadership?" I asked.

Mama CC expressed the difficulty in sharing with leadership. As she shared, inwardly I asked myself, *Why not share with leadership? Are they not in a position to encourage and counsel a congregate in their time of need?*

Mama CC shared that confidentiality was an issue. If members shared their concerns, it was certain to be heard over the pulpit Sunday morning.

"We really didn't feel safe to share with leadership, and most of the issues were deemed to be spiritual issues. All you were advised to do was pray," she said.

What did strike me as strange was that some of the past congregates worked in the mental health field. Is it safe to assume that there was a fear in sharing this knowledge, in offering some precepts of mental health counseling as a way of confronting some of the issues.

Come to think of it, if I was met with resistance in the 21st century, I can only imagine what resistance or rebuke they would have encountered. In those days, insight on mental health was not welcomed in the church.

As Mama CC continued with her narrative, my heart felt her sadness and disappointment. There were certainly many missed opportunities to foster healing and restoration to a church family experiencing so much pain.

Mental health and the church have been a long-standing issue within the church. Today there has been great strides in the integration of one's spirituality into the mental health profession to promote healing both physically, emotionally, and spiritually. For the church world, though, it has been somewhat of a slow go. Don't get me wrong, many churches are moving in that direction, and are more receptive to address mental health issues within their congregation.

Often people of faith tend to shy away from any form of psychology or psychotherapy, deeming it as secular by nature. When one does consider seeking therapy, it is often deemed as a lack of empathy for their own belief system. Some think that seeking therapy means abandoning their faith in favor of "secular" treatment. If a pastor or clergy seeks education in the field of psychology or psychotherapy, it is feared that they will forfeit their theological position. My experience as clergy and obtaining education in psychotherapy raised a few brows, more from who I would call "seasoned saints."

Listening to Mama CC's narrative, and performing research for my thesis, it became apparent that there have been some misconceptions and a lack of understanding regarding pastoral counseling and psychotherapy. I am not only speaking from personal experience but evidence-based research that supports the proven benefits and effectiveness of psychological approaches in pastoral counseling. If both biblical and today's pastoral counseling are applied appropriately it will only serve to enhance the counseling process, as it is all for the benefit of the client/congregate and for leadership, as well.

Maybe you will choose not to take my word for it, and that is okay. Maybe this concept is not for everyone, and that is perfectly fine. For me, it is my testimony as to where God has brought me from and through. This integrative approach served me well, so I feel compelled to share it with those who counsel their congregates and their families.

It's like hearing the good news of Jesus Christ—you just can't keep it to yourself. Oh, Mama CC, if only we had the knowledge and understanding as we do today of the positive impact of mental health on one's well-being!

As I have digressed a bit, I'll come back to the many studies that support the benefit of an integrative approach. What I want to express is my personal experience with this type of integration, how my healing and the healing of my family of origin came about.

Despite the dysfunction within my family of origin, I have endured. My grandmother covered me with her prayers. It was my grandmother who planted the seed of God's word and it was God who did the watering and drawing. Many a time I had nowhere to turn, but my grandmother taught me when life gets tough to turn to Jesus. Was it an easy road? No. There were plenty of bumps in the road and hills to climb. There were some very deep-seated issues that required healing. I shed many a tear on this healing journey, I felt alone and isolated, and like no one cared about the pain I endured. I bottled it up and closed the lid, so I thought.

I never realized just how much my trauma had changed my view of people and the world around me. Control and trust issues pretty much dominated my life. God knew that there was a need for a deeper understanding of how my family trauma was playing out in my life. It is through God's divine guidance coupled with therapy that I learned the *me* that God intended *me* to be. To God be all the glory.

TO GLEAN OR NOT TO GLEAN

"The Father of compassion and the God of all comfort, who comforts us in all our troubles, so that we can comfort those in any trouble with the comfort we ourselves receive from God" (2 Corinthians 1:4, New International Version).

You may question the theological support for such a union between biblical counseling and today's pastoral counseling, which includes behavioral science. But remember that Jesus took all to the cross—not just physical pain, but emotional and psychological pain as well. It is at Calvary over 2,000 years ago that Jesus took all our emotional pain and suffering. If God saves all my tears, He is a God who cares for the matters of the heart. God's word extends an invitation to cast all our cares upon Him, for He cares for us. God cares for the anxious heart, the troubled mind, the traumatic soul, and broken spirit.

It is not God's will that people endure abuse. Violence against any person is evil and must be confronted, and those individuals who hurt others are to be held accountable. As I looked to the cross and dwelled within God's word, it was there that my healing and deliverance happened.

When we feel overwhelmed and crippled with emotional pain, we can take comfort in the fact that the Bible gives specific instructions on how we might become more emotionally and spiritually healthy. We can also take solace in psychology which provides the insight into the emotional and mental dynamic of our experience(s). It provides us with tools to enact the Bible's directives.

There is nothing that I see in scripture that refutes therapy. The scripture that comes to mind is Proverbs 27:17 where we are to live in community with other believers, fostering a loving and growing relationship, helping others toward positive change. So, take heart, it is okay to have Jesus and therapy, too.

My main task as a pastoral counselor and a marriage and family therapist is to establish an authentic relationship and foster an environment of safety and security. I know firsthand what it feels like to live in an environment void of safety and security. I can empathize with having no one to turn to, living within a family unit and feeling so lonely. That is why I thrive on creating a sacred space where the client(s) or congregant(s) can experience more fully the peace and joy of God's presence. Working with the client(s) or congregate(s), we partner together in decentering from anxious and irrational thoughts. I rely on the divine resources God has made available to promote change and inner healing of those who enter the counseling/therapy room.

As individuals seek to find guidance and the courage to survive life's problems or crisis, there is a yearning to know that God can help during these difficult situations. Many turn to self-help and human wisdom during times of struggle, but on occasion this does not suffice. As a pastoral counselor/MFT I carefully guide the client(s) or congregate in all truth according to the word of God, also carefully gleaning from the concepts of Marriage and Family Therapy. It is the combination of both disciplines that brings healing and restoration not just to the individual(s) but to the family as well.

As a follower of Christ and a minister, my ministry should exemplify that of Jesus Christ. Jesus' ministry reached out to those who had physical ailments and emotional issues. His ministry offered hope, healing, and restoration to the broken spirit. Jesus summons those who are in despair with the words, *"Come to me, all you who are weary and burdened, and I will give you rest"* (Matthew 11:28, New International Version). During his ministry on earth, Jesus was drawn to some of the neediest places and people in and outside of his community. As a pastoral counselor/marriage and family therapist, I move with great conviction and passion, taking my ministry from the walls of the church out into the communities, ministering and counseling individuals and families who are suffering and in despair.

If you're still not convinced of the benefits of an integrative approach to counseling, let's look at what else the Bible says about such a union.

The Bible speaks to the human heart and its pain. *"He heals the brokenhearted and binds up their wounds"* (Psalm 147:3, New International Version). The psalmist attests to how good God has been to His people; God is a reliable source to turn to when one is experiencing hurt, grief, and trauma. My role as pastoral counselor and marriage and family therapist, as with biblical counseling, does not rely solely on behavioral change. With the kingdom of God being most relevant in counseling and any therapeutic work, the goal is to foster an inner change.

When I explore some of the techniques within some psychotherapy models, I notice various forms of spiritual practices such as meditation, breathing exercises, and reflection. There is also significant data that shows the need for psychotherapists to be knowledgeable and sensitive to the spiritual and religious beliefs of their clients.

A close look at the book of Psalms is applicable to human emotional experiences. The Psalms offers actual experiences and emotions, all the while maintaining an awareness of who God is and what it is to be human. When I share the Psalms with a client or congregate, I am sharing and speaking God's word.

They often present weariness and despair; the Psalms speaks to their own suffering and the God who can bring comfort in times of distress. *"The Sovereign Lord has given me a well-instructed tongue, to know the word that sustains the weary"* (Isaiah 50:4, New International Version). Here is God's servant, surrendering to the will of God for the sake of others. The words of the prophet are appropriate for us who minister the Word of God. It is our job as a pastoral counselor/therapist to utilize God's word to comfort the weary spirit and bring refreshment to the broken soul.

I so relate to the book of Psalms. I reflect on my childhood years as my grandmother was grooming me for what now is ministry. It was the book of Psalms that was first introduced to me. My grandmother knew it was the book of Psalms that would help me through the dysfunction of my family of origin. It was the book of Psalms that became my go-to when things got rough, more specifically Psalm 121, which says, *"I will lift up my eyes to the mountains, where does my help come from? My help comes from the Lord, the Maker of heaven and earth"* (New King James Version). Many days, I would find myself sitting on the floor looking out of the window reciting this Psalm. When life's stressors seem to be the course of the day, I find peace in looking to the hills. A picturesque view of the mountains out of my window inspires the recitations of the Psalms.

The Bible is the essential tool within any counseling process as well as the pastoral counseling context. The use of the Bible serves as the final authority within the counseling process, offering a bio-psycho-social-spiritual approach treating the whole man. As a pastoral counselor and marriage and family therapist, I utilize insights and principles derived from both theology and from marriage and family therapy.

You may have noticed that I often use the term "behavioral science," which deals with human actions and emotions and how they influence a person's decisions. It also includes psychology and related disciplines. Sounds reasonable, right? Then why do some clergy quiver at the word "science?" I'm not qualifying or disqualifying "science," that's another person's battle. But I am arguing the value of some of the behavioral sciences, more specifically for psychotherapy.

Consider with me for a moment the "sciences." It is the word of God which governs and is the basis of science. The psalmist pronounces that *the Earth is the Lord's and everything in it, the world, and all who live in it* (Psalm 24, New King James Version). The Psalmist shares that God can be found in everything. When we look at God's creation, the works of God's hands are done with such meticulousness, it is beyond belief. We stand in awe of its magnificence.

An author notes, "Psychological science can be a valid avenue to learning more about God and knowing God better, but it needs to be used properly, just as Christian theology can aid psychological science in knowing more about people."[1]

As a pastoral counselor/MFT, it is important for me to consider both forms of God's communication. God's word governing the world is the basis of *science*. Science's domain is to explore nature, a way of knowing and exploring God's creation. God's domain is in the spiritual world, for the Bible is the basis for *theology*. Rather than conflicting with one another, both have been complementary to each other. They both present different aspects of human experiences.

Another point of consideration is that all biblical texts were not written for mere entertainment, but to elicit change and transformation. Psychotherapy is similar. It is not an entertainment exercise. Its purpose is transformation and healing, as well. A vast amount of the spiritual and religious orientations is likely to offer interventions addressing an individual's existential anxieties. Any psychotherapeutic intervention which provides a deep level of exploration of the human psyche will eventually broach this spiritual realm.

Feeling a little better about "behavioral science? Okay, I will leave you to your thoughts.

---

[1] Everett L. Worthington Jr., *Coming to Peace With Psychology: What Christians Can Learn From Psychological Science* (Downers Grove, ILL: IVP Academic Press, 2010), 46.

A Family Affair

"The most important thing in the world is family and love."
—John Wooden

If you have not figured it out yet, my conviction and passion is for the healing and restoration of the family unit. Family bonds are so important. The love in families helps us get through the most disastrous times. Families serve to provide safety and love and the support needed to face the challenges that presents themselves daily. Where there is family there is love, or at the very least, there should be.

My family of origin certainly did not meet these criteria. There is no way that abuse and love can co-exist in the same environment. It is either one or the other, and in my family of origin it certainly wasn't the latter. Certainly not the family love that fosters deep respect, loyalty, and healthy attachments. My family of origin was characterized by intense conflict and abuse. There was no space to express thoughts and feelings without enduring some negative consequence.

When God blessed me with a family of my own, I was hell-bent (excuse my...) on creating a family that was perfect. Unfortunately, I did not have the tools nor the know how to construct such a harmonious environment. There were no models, references, standards, or blueprints to follow. It seemed virtually impossible with a past filled with emotional and sexual abuse, to avoid sexual acting out.

My relationships were filled with sexual dysfunction and devaluing. I was once called a "bitch" and treated as such. It is no wonder that I ended up emotionally and psychologically damaged. I had low self-worth, no voice, and no sense of identity. I walked through life with a spirit of offense. It certainly was difficult at times to see any silver lining in a life lined with darkness.

My siblings' relationships and marriages were all but harmonious, and dysfunctionality crossed over each generation. All our relationships were doomed to failure from the start.

Thank God, there is life after emotional and sexual abuse. This was not the end of my story, as there is an expected end. I asked myself, *How do I acquire the ties that binds a family together? How do I achieve that harmonious environment that is conducive to a healthy functioning family?*

As I am always clergy first, I looked straight to the Bible, God's word, where I find the truth and foundational principals relative to the family. My education in theology/biblical studies coupled with marriage and family therapy set me on a pathway of learning and healing simultaneously.

THAT'S WHAT THE BIBLE SAYS

God has given me a conviction and passion for the family, and this conviction led to my licensure in marriage and family therapy. Coming from a family of dysfunction, I can attest to the effects of the trauma associated with dysfunction. I have come to learn the importance of a healthy family dynamic for one's emotional and psychological wellbeing. A healthy family dynamic is imperative for healthy development both physically and emotionally. It is through and by the family that we begin the process of socialization, learning morals and values. Family serves as a strong support system and teaches us what it takes to survive and thrive in the world. A healthy family dynamic offers safety, security, and unconditional love as it was ordained to be.

As we look to the scriptures regarding family, the concept of family is extremely important in the Bible, as we see its inception in the very beginning. Genesis 1:28 tells of God's directive: "*God blessed them and said to them, 'Be fruitful and increase in number; fill the earth and subdue it'* (New King James Version).

The Bible begins with the biological family as the central social context of human life. The family is depicted throughout Scripture as the primary means of God's communication with human beings. It is a reality based not just on the physical aspect, but also encompasses the spiritual aspect. From a theological viewpoint, the Old Testament narrative and the New Testament narratives are quite strong in stressing the sanctity of the family. Theologically we are created for relationship with self, others, and God. When viewing the relational aspect within the scriptures, it is the family unit through which God perpetuates His covenant.

When pouring out His saving grace it is poured onto the entire family unit, sending a message of hope. God never disregarded the institution of family. Throughout the Old Testament and New Testament, even though God singled out an individual, He dealt with the individual in the context of family. In the story of Noah, for example, God not only extended grace to Noah, but also He extended grace to Noah's wife, children, and in-laws.

The family unit continues to be reinforced within the New Testament narrative. For example, in The Acts of the Apostles 11:14, the Apostle Peter brings God's message to the household of Cornelius and his entire household received salvation. Another example in scripture is Acts 16:15, where the Apostle Paul preached in Philippi, leading Lydia and her entire household to redemption and baptism of the entire family. Both testaments present the family as a physical and spiritual institution depicted in its ideal form, a prominent image of reconciliation and harmony.

When there is disharmony in the family, families seek out in desperation clergy or a therapist to deal with both the emotional, psychological, and spiritual issues. *"When hard pressed, I cried to the Lord; he brought me into a spacious place"* (Psalm 118:5, New King James Version). When a person cries out in pain and despair, God hears the cry and answers. When the heart is wounded and the spirit is broken, it is God and His word that becomes a reliable source to address the pain and brokenness of one's heart.

God has responded to my cries of despair. Tears are cathartic and the irrigation of the soul. The tears that I shed never hit the ground as God has them all close to His heart. I share my journey from victimhood, to taking accountability of my own happiness and joy. Having a sense of agency, control, and empowerment, it was time to turn the page, moving from trauma to triumph and share my testimony in hopes to encourage others that abuse is not the end of your story.

TO BE OR NOT TO BE/ SHOULD I, OR SHOULDN'T I?

As a pastoral counselor and MFT, I hold a unique position in my approach to family therapy. I can attend to family religion and spirituality in ways that can lead to the fostering of family cohesion and resilience.

I have grown to have a great appreciation for an approach that includes the spiritual and psychotherapy. I do not exclude, but include, meeting the needs of the cognitive abilities and spiritual belief. I do not have to forfeit my spirituality or theoretical orientation in offering a bio-psycho-social-spiritual approach in the counseling/ therapy room. I don't have to leave each discipline at the door, for if I do, I am doing my client(s)/congregate(s) a disservice.

As I had the opportunity to present this approach to some clergy members, some were receptive, but there were those that responded with some opposition. It wasn't a hard fast "No," but it was more of *how can you mix the two, and why would I consider such an approach?* Some drew a hard line between spirituality and psychotherapy, and I respect their choice. Any "challenge" relative to this approach can be met if handled both ethically and appropriately. There is little room for skepticism as this approach reinforces the theological perspective of the individual's presenting problem as well as the behavioral science relative to human action.

As a pastoral counselor and marriage and family therapist, I am more than what I do—it is who I am. I am a servant of Jesus Christ and a marriage and family therapist called to serve those individuals and families that are in pain. I pride myself in offering not only sound theological guidance, but also a professional level of mental health care to individuals and their families.

Whether the individuals are Christians or non-Christians, I don't see denominations. As a pastoral counselor, I see individuals as souls, and as a marriage and family therapist, I see individuals as relational beings. I rely on God to help me to see my clients through the eyes of Christ. My goal is to promote the healing of the whole man and bring healing, restoration to the entire family unit. Just as the mental health profession values the power of prayer and one's spirituality, as a pastoral counselor I value the approach to mental healthcare, drawing on the wisdom of psychology and the behavioral sciences.

Being a pastoral counselor/marriage and family therapist, I enter the world of the individual(s) or families' pain, incorporating sound biblical theology and appropriate therapeutic techniques. I take care in utilizing social and behavioral sciences in the counseling process, as misuse can potentially cause psychological and physical distress. Since the Bible serves as the authoritative text, I exercise careful exegesis to help those I minister to, doing no harm. I am intentional to render due beneficence and nonmaleficence toward those I serve.

As written in Deuteronomy 30:15, "*See, I have set before you today life and good, death and evil*" (New King James Version). Evil may have happened to me, but God gives us a choice of choosing life or death. I chose to live that I may show forth the love of God and share my story of moving from trauma to triumph.

Pastors, clergy, therapists, and counselors, God has equipped us with what is needed to minister to those who are living in the pains of the past. We not only have His word, but we also have the therapeutic interventions available to promote healing to the whole man. I found it advantageous to include family, partners, spouses within my treatment protocols. With this approach the individual is not treated in a bubble but with a bio-psycho-social-spiritual approach within a system, *the family.*

THE FAMILY MATTERS

*"Now all things are of God, who has reconciled us to Himself through Jesus Christ, and has given us the ministry of reconciliation......
and has committed to us the word of reconciliation"*
(2 Corinthians 5:18-19, NKJV).

Throughout the Old and New Testaments, God's mission is of restoration, redemption, and salvation with the fulfillment through and by His son Jesus Christ. God's entire plan of salvation is built on the premise of reconciliation, reconciling all of creation back to Himself through relationship.

The family was the first institution God created. Through family, God illustrates visibly the relationship which exists between Christ and His church. It is through family God sought to bring into relationship the world with Himself. The family is the basis in God's plan, that is why the enemy seeks to destroy it.

Family reconciliation brings joy, healing, and renewed attachments. This is God's desire and the work of the Cross. I think of all the brokenness in my family of origin. There were certainly cut-offs, lack of respect, and an environment void of love and nurturing. We were a family in need of renewed and secured attachments.

A family that lacks respect and honor for one another only serves to be a breeding ground for brokenness and high levels of dysfunction, which was the dynamic of my family of origin in a nutshell. How

I wish my family of origin understood the importance of a healthy family dynamic! A healthy family dynamic would have provided the love and respect needed for wholesome living. Unfortunately, both my mother and father entered into their marriage with their own unresolved issues, which precipitated an environment of dysfunction.

The symptoms of dysfunction were to be my demise, but God meant it for good. For what was to destroy me fostered resilience, and that which was to weaken gave strength. What was to result in indifference led to compassion; a compassion for those who have suffered by the hand of family dysfunction. God took the very fabric of my being and reworked it, as there is a distinct plan and purpose for my life. When I could no longer navigate the perils of the day, it was the Lord God that navigated me through the storms of life. God became the compass that orients me and provides divine direction.

I no longer live in the darkness of pain and despair. I cannot go through life looking in the rearview mirror of the past, I must look forward to where God is taking me. To move forward from the past, peace must be made with the past. For me, forgiving had to be learned, as unforgiveness kept me chained to the past. Unforgiveness is all I knew. How do you learn to love those that hurt you? I had to forgive to love again, love again so I could forgive.

I often wonder if my life was void of all the abuse and hardships, would I be where I am today, in a life where Christ is the center of my very being? Only God knows for sure. My story now has a song, a song of triumph as now that which is before me is greater than what's behind me. I continue to strive for a deeper relationship with God—for He has always had one with me—and a continued focus on my mental wellness.

A LITTLE RESEARCH NEVER HURTS ANYONE

A personal testimony with a sprinkle of research can be a recipe for a solid defense, a defense for an integrated approach that is a union of theology and psychotherapy. Here is a little research (excerpts from my theses titled *"Biblical Pastoral Counseling: An Integrative Approach to Healing,"* published 2022) to support my advocacy of an integrative approach to healing, along with a focus on the family.

As a pastoral counselor and marriage and family therapist, the approach I utilize not only consists of the client's biology, psychology, and family of origin, but also on the client's entire ego system. When I speak of an ego system relative to family, it depicts families as a closely related social group that interacts with their environment. We cannot treat individuals in a bubble, as that would be a disservice to the congregate/client and the family. I do not treat the IP (individual patient) alone. Including the family is crucial for the success of any therapeutic process. Family support lends itself to treatment satisfaction and increased congregate/client participation.

Pastoral counselors understand the human condition, focusing on themes relating to life and death, freedom, limitations, being, and becoming. We understand how the client views God may greatly influence how they view themselves. Also, how they perceive distress, make sense of their suffering, and cope with their circumstances. If the client views God as a lawgiver or judge, the client may struggle with guilt or feel they are always on trial, versus one who views God as merciful, loving, and full of grace.

Another point to consider is how God's word will ultimately form the pastoral counselor's views, understanding of human condition, and practice.

The Bible is not a psychological book, nor does it contain theoretical terms, but the Bible does speak to the matters of the heart and its many pains and to the human condition. The Bible speaks with authority about thoughts and emotions and about pathological problems, such as anxiety, depression, anger, and mental health disorders. When it comes to counseling, marriage and family therapist and pastoral counselors share more commonalities than differences, as both disciplines focus on conflict resolution, life adaptation, and behavioral and relational issues.

With the various principles of the pastoral counseling process, it is anticipated that a systemic integrative approach will result in long-term success and effective results. Pastoral counselors hold a unique position in the field of counseling. One of the most appealing attributes is the emphasis on the congregates/clients' potential. Their present experiences, values, and spiritual dimension form a basis for a holistic intervention. Pastoral counselors bring a uniqueness to the model. They are skilled in theology, proficient in exegesis, and clinical expertise. Their expertise goes beyond the walls of the church into communities, providing pastoral care to those individuals in need.

As a best practice, pastoral counselors take care in utilizing the social and behavioral sciences in the counseling process, with the understanding that any misuse can bring psychological harm to the client.

The pastoral counselor brings not only the spiritual and theological components to address the family issue, but also a family-systems approach that can help families dealing with mental health issues. It is marriage and family therapy that provides a systems approach, exploring the elements of the family system. This approach helps the congregate/client resolve the presenting problem in the context of their family.

Families work within a social system. Family members interact to influence each other's behavior and they are intensely connected emotionally. Family systems theory improves family dynamics. This dynamic develops healthy boundaries, improves communications, and improves the family's problem-solving abilities.

A family systems approach allows the pastoral counselor to view the family system rather than individual elements. This approach is beneficial in treating mental health and behavioral health issues of depression, anxiety, substance abuse, and impulse control. These are the most common disorders that present themselves for pastoral counseling.

The pastoral counselor uses a contextual approach. This approach considers the primary symptom, social factors, and emotional factors, with a focus on the family's deficits and strengths. Including the family within the counseling process contributes to the well-being and the mental health of the individual and the family.

The pastoral counselor comprehends the human existence as being created as relational beings with the possibility of relationships with oneself, others, and God, and the power of human relationships in the healing process.

A marriage and family therapist understands the significance of including the family within the counseling process. This inclusion contributes to the well-being and the mental health of the individual and the family.

There are theoretical and empirical connections between religion, spirituality, mental health, science, reason, and faith. One's spirituality can affect one's mental health, just as one's mental health can affect one's spirituality. Each are in harmony with each other relative to one's cognition, emotions, and behavior. It is the task of the pastoral counselor to glean and integrate insights from medicine, psychology, the Bible, and theology, to understand mental illness and to help others recover from it.

Pastoral counselors have a unique relationship that goes beyond the counseling room. Fostering a healthy therapeutic relationship enables the pastoral counselor to find opportunities for religious and spiritual integration. Often when an individual seeks out pastoral counseling, there is a need that goes beyond a "diagnosis." Most clients are seeking a deeper meaning. When a pastoral counselor engages in the congregates spirituality and the search for meaning of life, this intervention aligns with existential humanistic intervention. This can answer the broader questions that goes beyond the perceived diagnosis. This approach emphasizes the importance of human choices and decisions, allowing the congregate or client to develop meaning and value within their lives, just as health professionals do.

If you have gotten this far into my story, I first want to say thank you. Second, I pray that you can see and appreciate the value of an integrated approach to counseling. Through testimony and research,

I pray I have provided a solid defense in support of an integrative approach, a value-added approach that combines pastoral counseling and marriage and family therapy. It will be a welcomed experience to those who cross the threshold of the counseling room.

A FAMILY WHO PRAYS TOGETHER, HEALS TOGETHER

A TESTAMENT OF TRUTH

I have come to understand that God can and will use one individual as a catalyst for change.

I witnessed this manifestation within my family of origin. One by one, my family of origin began to seek the Lord for healing of their own internal struggles. What is visible today is a reworking, and one by one, God is healing and reconciling us as a family unit. God is fulfilling the promise of saving our very household.

There are no longer walls of defense or the spirit of offense, there is a crumbling as the walls of Jericho. We are now a family that prays together, giving us the opportunity to heal together. Our individual traumas and journeys are unique to each of us. Our paths, as unique as they are, lead to a common ground and that is reconciliation. Our family landscape has certainly changed. It is now fertile ground, a ground that is right for healing to take place. It's a family affair as we continue to work at fostering a more cohesive and healthy family relationship. It is through the power of love and nurture that heals our broken soul and spirit.

As noted, Biblical scripture places a high emphasis on the family, making family one of God's masterpieces. Jesus came as God in the flesh, being born in the context of family. It was through the nurturing care and guidance from his family that Jesus grew in wisdom and stature. (Luke 2:52, New International Version).

Taking my conviction and passion for the family to heart, I bring this conviction to those I hold close and those I serve. As clergy, my first ministry must be to my family, which serves as a prerequisite for ministry—after God, of course.

FINAL APPEAL

When the family unit lacks the emotional connection that binds a family together, it is quite common for members to seek this connection elsewhere. We will instinctually seek the closeness of others, as we are created as relational beings. We search for self-validation and self-worth. We find identity in tangible things, all in futile efforts to bolster our self-esteem and self-worth. As we seek to fill the voids left by dysfunction, we fall for the things that resemble that connection and nurturance that we so desire. But all too often it never satisfies, it only disappoints. Seeking only lends itself to exasperate those underlying insecurities, resonating feelings of rejection.

This yearning grows daily as we struggle to find our place in the world. All our efforts yield very little success. We begin to gravitate to anything that will bring solace to this deep yearning, regardless of the cost. It is not until we come to understand that this yearning is purpose, that we can then find rest. It is only when we recognize that our identity lies in the Savior that we will find clear direction and purpose in life.

It is here that I make my final appeal for a systemic integrated approach to all who serve in a pastoral counseling and therapeutic role.

As a pastoral counselor and marriage and family therapist, I exercise an approach that has been proven effective in healing and restoration to the whole individual and their family.

Who would have thought that God could use evil for good? God can take all our pain and trauma and make it the foundation of one's ministry. Let us consider the value of an integrative systemic approach, one that takes into consideration one's entire being in the context of family.

As pastoral counselors, we recognize the connection between people and family. No one person lives or acts in isolation, no one is an island within themselves. We are all affected by one another's behaviors because we are intrinsically connected to one another. The family is a divine institution, the primary agent in teaching values, resilience, and socialization. It's the family that supplies the emotional and psychological support to its members. To dismiss the family from any therapeutic process would only serve to be a disservice to the client/congregate and to the family as well.

We as pastors, counselors, and therapists are equipped in helping our congregates/clients in achieving not only spiritual wellness but mental wellness as well. In so doing, we as helping professionals never have to worry about forfeiting our pastoral orientation.

As pastoral counselors and therapists, we serve as the bridge between brokenness to wholeness, with Jesus serving as the girders, the most essential part of any bridge. Come, let us reason together, let us consider an integrative approach to the healing of one family at a time; moving families from trauma to triumph.

The scars of trauma run into the deepest part of our being, but it doesn't define who we are.

BIBLIOGRAPHY

Alexander, Desmond, T. and Brain Rosner, D.A. Carson, Graeme Goldsworthy. *New Dictionary of Biblical Theology: Exploring the Unity and Diversity of Scripture.* Downers Grove, IL: InterVarsity Press, 2000.

Alton, Gord. "Toward an Integrative Model of Psychospiritual Therapy: Bringing Spirituality and Psychotherapy Together." *Journal of Pastoral Care & Counseling* (2020):159-165. Accessed February 26, 2021. http://www.journals.sagepub.com/home/pcc/vol.74(3).

Amy Norton, "America's Stigma Against Depression May Finally be Fading." *Health Day,* (2021):2, accessed February 20, 2022. https://www.nami.org.

American Association of Pastoral Counselors-National Action Alliance, https://theactionalliance.org.

American Psychiatric Association Foundation. *Mental Health: A Guide for Faith Leaders.* Arlington, VA. American Psychiatric Association Foundation, 2016. https://www.psychiatry.org.

Benz, Johnathan, and Kristina Robb-Dover. *The Recovery-Minded Church: Loving and Ministering to People with Addiction.* Downers, Grove, IL., InterVarsity Press, 2016.

Brewer, Judson, *"Treatment Anxiety: We've Got Anxiety All Wrong."* Psychology Today, July/August 2021.

Campbell-Lane, Yvonne, Lotter, George *Biblical Counselling regarding Inner Change*, North-West University, 2005.

Carp-Heseltine, William and Matthew Hoskins. "Clergy as a Front-line Mental Health Services: A UK Survey of Medical Practitioners and Clergy." National Institutes of Health (2020): Accessed February 19, 2022. http://www.ncbi.nim.nih.gov.

Center for Substance Abuse Treatment and family therapy. "Treatment Improvement Protocol (TIP) Series No. 39.". Substance Abuse and Mental Health Services Administration (US). Rockville MD: 2004. www.ncbi.nim.nih.gov.

Clinton, Tim and Ron Hawkins. *The Popular Encyclopedia of Christian Counseling: An indispensable Tool for Helping People with Their Problems.* Eugene, Oregon, Harvest House Publishers, 2011.

Cook, Christopher C.H., "Mental Health in the Kingdom of God." *Sage Journal* (2020): 2-15. Accessed June 29, 2021. https://journal.sagepub.com/doi/full.

Cook, Sonya, "Biblical Pastoral Counseling: An Integrative Approach to Healing" *Scholars Crossing* (2022) Accessed September 19, 2023. https://digitalcommons.liberty.edu/doctoral/3493.

Coyle, Suzanne, M., "Pastoral Caring Through Spiritual Narratives: Uncovering Spiritual Narratives. *Using Story in Pastoral Care and Ministry.*" http://ezproxy.liberty.edu/login?url=https:11.

Epperly, Bruce. *A Center In The Cyclone: Twenty-First Century Clergy Self-Care.* Lanham, MD: Rowman & Littlefield Publishers, 2014.

Erwin, Kathie. "The Heart of Trauma Counseling." *Christian Counseling Today.* Vol. 25, NO. 1, 54.

Flores, Ricky. "Calvary Baptist Church in Haverstraw Reopens After Repairs." *The Journal News.* October 25, 2015. https://www.lohud.com.

Focht, Carali. "The Joseph Story: A Trauma-Informed Biblical Hermeneutic for Pastoral Care Provider." *Pastoral Psychology* (2020):209-223. Accessed December 11, 2020. https://doi.org/10.1007/s11089-020-00901-w.

Gill, Jesse, W. "Attachment Bonds and Safety: The Antidote to Trauma." Christian Counseling Today, Vol. 25, No. 1.

Goger, Pauline and Robin Weersing. "Family Based treatment of anxiety disorders: A Review of the Literature." *Journal of Marriage and Family therapy.* (2010-2019): Accessed February 16, 2022. https://pubmed.ncbi.nih.gov/34424998.

Gordon, Joshua A. "One Year In: COVID-19 and Mental Health." *National Institute of Mental Health* (2021): 1-4. Accessed February 20, 2022. http://www.nimh.nih.gov/about/director/messages/2021/one-year-in-covid-19.

Gotter, Anna. "Behavioral Therapy: Definition, Types, and Effectiveness." *Health Line.* (2018) Accessed February 17, 2022. https://www.healthline.com/health/behavioral-therapy.

Growne, Julia, Corinne Cather and Kim T. Mueser. "Common Factors in Psychotherapy." *Oxford Research Encyclopedias.* (2021). https://www.oxforde.com/psychology/view/10.1093/acrefore.

Heshmat, Shahram. "Resilience." *Psychology Today* (2004): 1. Accessed September 10, 2021. https://www.psychology.com.

Issler, Klaus. *Living into the Life of Jesus: The Formation of Christian Character.* Downer Grove, IL: InterVarsity Press, 2012.

James, John, W., and Russell Friedman. *The Grief Recovery Handbook.* New York, N.Y: Harper Collins Books. 2009.

Klan, Wefner, RA. "He heals the Broken and Binds Up their Wounds (Psalm 147:3) Perspectives on Pastoral Care." *Scholarly Journals* (2012): 1-12. Accessed December 11, 2020. https://search-proquest-com.ezproxy.liberty.edu/docview/vol/iss/4/.

Koenig, Harold, G. "Current Research Trends Regarding Best Clinical Practices for Trauma Care." *Christian Counseling Today*, vol. 24, No.1.

Lawrence, Michael. *Biblical Theology in The Life of The Church: A Guide for Ministry.* Wheaton IL: Crossway, 2010.

Lotter, George, and Yvonne Campbell-Lane. "Biblical Counselling Regarding Inner Change". *School of Ecclesiastical Sciences* (2005):

99-102. Accessed September 2021. https://www.koersjournal. org.

Mandley, Anita. The Legacy of Historical Trauma: Grasping the Larger Story. *Psychotherapy Networker*. September/October 2020.

Maynard, Elizabeth, A. and Jill I. Snodgrass. *Understanding Pastoral Counseling*. New York, N.Y: Springer Publishing Company, 2015.

McDaniel, Susan, H., William J. Doherty and Jeri Hepworth. *Medical Family Therapy and Integrated Care*. Washington D.C.: American Psychological Association, 2014.

McDonald, Ron. *Building the Therapeutic Sanctuary: The Fundamentals of Psychotherapy from a Pastoral Counseling Perspective*. Bloomington, IN: Author House, 2000.

Mizock, Lauren. "4 Ways Culture Impacts Acceptance of Mental Health Problems: Cultural Factors in the Road to Recovery." Psychology Today (2017):1-6. Accessed February 20, 2022. https://www.psychologytoday.com.

Noonan, Susan, J. "Mental Illness Splits Families: How to Avoid Losing Your Family."*Psychology Today*. (2017): 1-8. Accessed February 20, 2022. https://www.psychologytoday.com.

North, William, Jr. "The American Association of Pastoral Counselors: Advancing theory and professional practice scholarly and reflective publications. "*Journal of Pastoral Care. & Counseling*. (1998): 2. Accessed on February 18, 2022. http://doi.org/10.11 77/002234098804200302.

Norton, Amy. "America's Stigma Against Depression May Finally be Fading." *Health Day* (2021): 2. Accessed February 20, 2022. https://www.nami.org.

Pan, Der, Jen, Peter, Liang-Yu F. Deng, Shiou Ling Tsai and Jenny S.S. Yuan. "Issues of Integration in Psychological Counseling Practices from Pastoral Counseling Perspective." *Journal of Psychology and Christianity* no.2 (2013): 146-159. Accessed February 18, 2022. https://psycnet.apa.org/record/2013-30984-005/vol.32.

Rait, Douglas R. "The Therapeutic Alliance in Couples and Family Therapy." JCLP/In Session: Psychotherapy in Practice. (2000):211-224. Accessed September 29, 2021. https://.www.researchgate.net/publication/12596519/, Vol. 56(2).

Randall, Rebecca. "Today's Pastoral Counseling Is More Fluent in Psychology." *Christianity Today.* (2021). Accessed October 19, 2021. http://www.christianitytoday.com.

Ryken, Leland, James C. Wilhoit and Tremper Longman III. *Dictionary of Biblical Imagery: An Encyclopedic Exploration of the Images, Symbols Motifs, Metaphors, Figures of Speech and Literary Patterns of the Bible.* Downers, Grove, IL: Inter-Varsity Press, 1998.

SAMHSA. "Risk and Protective Factors". *Substance Abuse and Mental Health Services Administration.* (2019). Accessed October 19, 2021. https://www.samhsa.gov.

Searchy, Nelson. "Becoming Who You Want to be: How to Reclaim Physical, Spiritual, Mental and Emotional Health." Christian Counseling Today. Vol. 24, No. 2.

Silvestri, Kenneth. "It is All About Relationships: What Family Therapist Should Know and Consider About Their Approach." Family Therapy Magazine, September/October 2020.

Snodgrass, Jill L. "The Future of Spiritually Integrated Psychotherapy in the AAPC Tradition." *Journal of Pastoral Care & Counseling.* (2019): 153-156. Accessed February 15, 2022. http://www.pubmed.ncbi.nim.nih.gov.

Stephens, Rachel, and William I. Hathaway. "Addressing Integrative Issues in the Service Delivery of Trauma Care." Christian Counseling Today. Vol. 24 no.1.28.

Tracy, Steven R. *Mending the Soul: Understanding and Healing Abuse.* Grand Rapids, MI: Zondervan, 2005.

Vaughn, Bruce Rogers. "Best Practices in Pastoral Counseling: Is Theology Necessary?" *The Journal of Pastoral Theology* 23 (1) (2013):

1-24. Accessed September 11, 2019. https://www.researchgate.net.

Walker, Reid, Kathryn, Scheidegger, Tammy H., End, Laurel, Amundsen, Mark. *The Misunderstood Pastoral Counselor: Knowledge and Religiosity as Factors Affecting a Client's Choice.* Article 62, 2012. https://www.counseling.org.

Waters, Susan, E. *Addiction and Pastoral Care.* Grand Rapids MI: Wm B. Eerdmans Publishing Co., 2019.

World Health Organization. "Mental Health: Strengthening Our Response." (2018). Accessed October 19, 2021. https://www.who.int/news-room/fact-sheets.

Worthington, Everett, L. *Coming to Peace with Psychology: What Christians Can Learn From Psychological Science.* Downers Grove, IL., InterVarsity Press, 2010.